Hoshin Kanri for Healthcare

Toyota-Style Long-Term Thinking and
Strategy Deployment to Unlock Your
Organization's True Potential

Hoshin Kanri for Healthcare

Toyota-Style Long-Term Thinking and Strategy Deployment to Unlock Your Organization's True Potential

Jerry Berlanga
Brock Husby
Heather K. Anderson
With contributions from Debra McClendon

Routledge
Taylor & Francis Group

A PRODUCTIVITY PRESS BOOK

Routledge
Taylor & Francis Group
711 Third Avenue, New York, NY 10017

© 2018 by Jerry Berlanga, Brock Husby, and Heather K. Anderson
Routledge is an imprint of Taylor & Francis Group, an Informa business

No claim to original U.S. Government works

Printed on acid-free paper

International Standard Book Number-13: 978-1-138-58059-6 (Hardback)
International Standard Book Number-13: 978-1-4987-8499-3 (Paperback)
International Standard Book Number-13: 978-1-315-15569-2 (eBook)

**Visit the Taylor & Francis Web site at
http://www.taylorandfrancis.com**

**and the Productivity Press site at
http://www.ProductivityPress.com**

To my loving wife, Bonnie, who continues to inspire me; my late mother, Pauline, who dedicated her life to our family; and the hardworking, compassionate, caring, and dedicated physicians, nurses, administrators, and staff that take care of all of us each day.

Jerry Berlanga

To Prof. Jeffrey K. Liker, who, throughout my education and career, has continuously inspired, challenged, and matured my understanding of Lean and the Toyota Production System; and to the dedicated leaders, staff, and physicians of Guadalupe Regional Medical Center (GRMC) and other partner healthcare organizations, who on a daily basis remind me of why I love doing the work I do through their passion, dedication, and focus on serving patients, the community, and society as a whole.

Brock Husby, PhD, PE

First and foremost, to my wonderful husband, children, mother, and siblings, who have always encouraged and supported me. Second, to the incredible people I worked with and for at the Baptist Health System, whose compassion for others and drive for continuous improvement have always been an inspiration to me. Lastly, in memory of my stepfather, Bill, who took me in as his own and was my biggest fan.

Heather K. Anderson

Contents

List of Figures

List of Tables

About the Authors

 **Jerry Berlanga** has more than 20 years of Lean Six Sigma and change management experience, and has led and supported Lean Six Sigma transformations with key organizations, such as CPS Energy, United Services Automobile Association, Baylor Scott & White Healthcare, and CHRISTUS Health, and other leading organizations across the United States and Canada, such as UMass Memorial, Alpena General, Alliance Imaging, and Ontario Health Quality Council. As Associate Vice President (AVP) of Lean Healthcare Strategies, Jerry supported the Lean transformation of Baylor Scott & White Healthcare. He is currently the system director of performance improvement at CHRISTUS Health, supporting performance improvement transformation.

Jerry is a respected Lean Six Sigma teacher, coach, mentor, and author. He earned his MS degree in systems and engineering management from Texas Tech University. He currently coteaches a one-day Lean daily management and Lean fundamentals workshop at the University of Texas at San Antonio (UTSA). Jerry founded UTSA's continuous improvement professionals group several years ago to bring Lean Six Sigma professionals together to share innovations, best practices, and advances in Lean Six Sigma, and create mentorships, internships, and job opportunities for junior Lean coaches and engineers. Jerry invites readers to e-mail him at jerry@leanproviders.com to learn more about Hoshin Kanri and Lean daily management.

 **Brock Husby, PhD, PE**, is a process improvement leader who has multi-industry experience in holistically integrating Lean across manufacturing, transactional, facility design, service, and other contexts to advance the field of Lean and the Toyota Production System. This broad experience empowers organizations to truly revolutionize their value streams from product development to customer delivery. This approach delivers exceptional results that drive positive culture change and high return on investment outcomes. He focuses on deeply understanding where an organization is currently at, developing a customized approach to match its needs, and "leading from the front" through facilitation, training, gemba observation, and executive and frontline coaching. This approach is grounded in evidence-based Lean and Toyota Production System principles that go beyond the normal Lean projects and tool-based approaches to drive meaningful and sustained change. Brock is a Licensed Professional Engineer (PE), certified Lean coach, consultant, author (Productivity Press, Inc. and Institute of Industrial and Systems Engineers [IISE]), instructor (IISE, Engineering Lean Six Sigma [ELSS], and the University of Texas at San Antonio), speaker, and researcher. Brock worked as a process assurance engineer and corrective actions engineer for the space shuttle program at the Kennedy Space Center (Cape Canaveral, Florida), a consultant in the automotive service parts industry, and a technical assistant at *Car and Driver* magazine. Brock was an associate vice president at Baylor Scott & White Health, where he was an integral part of the deployment of a holistic Lean approach throughout the 13-hospital, 13,000-employee system. A case study from Brock's PhD dissertation (based on his professional work) was recently featured in Prof. Jeff Liker's new book, *The Toyota Way to Service Excellence* (McGraw-Hill, 2016). Brock was one of the three industrial engineers who built the program for Denver Health, becoming the first healthcare delivery organization to win the coveted Shingo Prize for Operational Excellence (March 2011), and demonstrated operational expense savings of $124 million (as of 2013). Brock holds a BSE, MSE, and PhD in industrial and operations engineering from the University of Michigan, Ann Arbor.

Heather K. Anderson has greater than 20 years of experience in healthcare finance, operations, and performance improvement. Almost 10 years, Heather worked with the Baptist Health System in San Antonio, Texas, in various system leadership roles, including vice president of quality and performance management. Heather was responsible for system quality, operational improvement, accreditation, risk management, infection prevention, transitional care, and business analytics. She was also responsible for the Lean operations of the system, which included development of the daily management structure, kaizen events, strategy deployment, and Lean training and education.

Before joining Baptist, Heather was at Memorial Hermann Healthcare System in Houston, Texas, for more than eight years in various roles, including director of financial operations, Medicare profitability, and organization effectiveness. Prior to that, she worked in financial operations for Columbia HCA Bayshore Medical Center. She received her bachelor of arts degree from the University of Texas at Austin and her master of business administration/master of healthcare administration from the University of Houston–Clear Lake. Prior to entering healthcare, Heather worked in nuclear chemistry at Los Alamos National Laboratory, where she was first exposed to a high-reliability infrastructure. Heather has also served as adjunct faculty for the Baptist School of Health Professions, teaching healthcare performance and process improvement for the BS in Healthcare Management Program. Heather is a certified Lean Six Sigma master black belt with a concentration in Lean systems.

Debra McClendon is currently the director of learning and development and executive coach at a wealth-management organization. Before that, she spent 18 years in Toyota's Information Systems Division, 12 of which were as a technology manager and 11 as a talent development manager at Toyota Motors North America. She earned an MA in organizational leadership from Biola University in La Mirada, California; an MA in human development from Fielding Graduate University in Santa Barbara, California; and a PhD in human and organizational systems from Fielding Graduate University. She is also a certified trainer on Toyota Business Practice and a certified trainer on Toyota's Ji-Kotei-Kanketsu and has been fully trained on Toyota's Hoshin process. In her spare time, she studies the brain and volunteers her time as an EEG neurofeedback technician.

Introduction

by Debra McClendon, PhD

This book provides an easy-to-read, step-by-step method to develop and implement Hoshin Kanri (also known as Hoshin planning) in healthcare. The authors have extensive knowledge, experience, and expertise in teaching Hoshin and Lean daily management (LDM) techniques in the healthcare industry. I have 28 years of experience working for Toyota, where Hoshin and the Toyota Production System (TPS) are well established. The authors look at Hoshin from a holistic perspective, recognizing the importance of traditional Hoshin tools and strategic planning models, while integrating concepts from value science and neuroscience to enhance the efficiency and effectiveness of the Hoshin journey. Toyota is a leader in the development and implementation of Hoshin Kanri. To begin with, I will recount my own experience at Toyota and what it was like living with Hoshin and other global content from inside the company. Then we will proceed to the subsequent chapters.

Chapter 1 outlines the "Lean journey" that any organization can take and the mindset that is needed to shift from a facilitative approach to a team approach in order to develop Hoshin (Hoshin Kanri translated into English means "direction" and "administration," respectively, and is often referred to as compass management). The author of this chapter discusses the benefits of understanding the meanings behind the whys of doing Hoshin, emphasizing the importance of being proactive rather than reactive in problem solving.

Chapter 2 provides an overview of a well-known goal-setting framework called SMART goals. In this chapter, the author describes how to translate strategic organizational goals into meaningful tasks, providing early warning signals for leaders to help keep the strategic plan on track. Several practical examples are provided to help the reader understand how to negotiate meaningful goals during a meeting in which leaders are tossing ideas back and forth to negotiate company goals. This technique is called *catch-ball*, a term used in the Hoshin process, borrowed from a children's game in which a ball is tossed from one child to the next. In the catch-ball process, ideas are tossed from person to person.

Chapter 3 continues the discussion on tracking and managing the goals that were set at the beginning of the Hoshin journey, but goes deeper into how to achieve those goals by utilizing visual aids and key leadership techniques to encourage the team members to stay on track with their goals.

Chapter 4 takes Hoshin planning onto the hospital floor and into hospital administration, where the operational work takes place. There is a focus in this chapter on team problem solving, with a reminder that continuous problem solving means continuously communicating with your fellow team members and your supervisors not only to ensure that the plan is progressing, but also to check on the team's motivation and morale. The chapter ends with a comprehensive look at the 11 steps to linking Hoshin planning to your LDM system.

Chapter 5 provides a firsthand look at a Lean management system model utilized by the Baptist Health System (BHS), which is located in San Antonio, Texas. BHS is a compassionate healthcare system that lives by its mission and values in everything it does. It is focused on providing the highest-quality care, and has done so by creating a culture of continuous improvement and increasing staff engagement at all levels of the organization. This chapter shares the BHS story through the experiences of one of its leaders, Heather Anderson, who was in charge of performance management for the system. In particular, the plan, process, lessons learned, integration of LDM into the plan, and strategy behind the plan are what make the BHS daily management system unique.

Heather has a master of business administration/master of healthcare administration from the University of Houston at Clear Lake. She provides a professional view of the Hoshin process, since she has almost 20 years of experience in healthcare finance, operations, and performance improvement in various system leadership roles, including vice president of quality and performance management at the BHS.

Chapter 6 presents general timelines that are typically deployed during the Hoshin process, from the executive (or C-suite) level all the way down to the frontline supervisors and staff members. These timelines bring all the levels together to participate in the ownership of the catch-ball process.

Chapter 7 presents what is needed to make the Hoshin plan a reality and how that process is managed through Hoshin change management (HCM) techniques. The author repeatedly emphasizes the importance of individual pride, friendly competition, and the daily measurement of key performance indicators (KPIs). There is a focus in this final chapter on building relationships between all the parties involved in the catch-ball process to ensure its efficiency and effectiveness and to guarantee that the process overwhelms no staff members. In fact, the people side of the Hoshin journey is undeniably one of its most important elements.

Respect for People

There is a lot of talk in LDM environments about putting people first. However, many companies are not sure what that means or how to accomplish it, although many companies have achieved some success with this focus. Globally, Toyota is by far the company that has made the most impact in this area. Toyota embraces problems and encourages its employees to look for problems in their daily work in order to continuously improve the workplace and its products. In healthcare, problems in capacity or care delivery can result in the loss of life. Therefore, the contributors to this book decided to step outside of healthcare for just a moment to explore an innovative approach to solving problems associated with the people side of Hoshin as experienced by a previous Toyota employee.

Neuro-Hoshin and the Neuroscience of Lean Management

Neuro-Hoshin and the *neuroscience of Lean management* (NLM) are terms coined by the present writer, who is a 28-year employee of Toyota Motors North America (TMNA). NLM is a concept that shows how neuroscience can be applied to LDM to stimulate the type of quality thinking that Toyota employees are expected to include in their daily work processes and documentation. Neuro-Hoshin, on the other hand, is a component of NLM that focuses on the *people side of Hoshin* and *three distinct areas* (workplace direction, Hoshin plan development, and the catch-ball process) where value science and neuroscience are applied to the Hoshin process to increase its efficiency. Both concepts support execution of the Hoshin plan from an intrinsic (pull) perspective rather than a systemic (push) perspective.

This author believes that these concepts are needed to ensure the overall effectiveness of Lean leadership and a successfully executed Hoshin.

Personal Note from Debra McClendon

The Toyota DNA was infused into my fellow team members and me during the many years that we worked for Toyota. While I would not refer to myself as a resident Hoshin expert at Toyota, I would agree that my love for the company and my personal quest to transform the hearts and minds of its employees stimulated my interest in incorporating value science and neuroscience into every aspect of Toyota's learning and development programs for which I was responsible. This introduction discusses Neuro-Hoshin and its role within NLM as shared from my personal experiences with Hoshin Kanri while I was working at Toyota. I describe my journey to understand the people side of Hoshin in order to close a gap that I noticed in Toyota's way of implementing Hoshin and other Toyota Way principles and concepts. The concepts described here are derived solely from my own personal experiences and scholarly research, and do not represent the views and opinions of Toyota Motor Corporation (TMC), TMNA, or any of its affiliates.

Personal Experience of Debra McClendon

Understanding what makes people tick and how to turn that tick into lasting change and personal effectiveness is a passion of mine that followed me to Toyota. Believe it or not, I had worked at Toyota for 12 years before I even encountered Hoshin Kanri or the Toyota Way principles, which are the foundation for Hoshin. This encounter occurred quite by accident in 2001, as I was having a dialogue with the then vice president of the North American Parts Division about how I might be able to make a difference at Toyota and advance my career. In the middle of our conversation, he pulled out a thin booklet that had the words *Toyota Way 2001* written on the front, and told me that this booklet was the blueprint to every job process at the company. He further explained that if I followed that blueprint in everything I did at Toyota, I would make a difference and my work would have meaning.

As I held that booklet in my hands, I marveled at it as if it were a diamond ring, for its value was uniquely special to me. The copy of the booklet that he showed me was a black-and-white xerox copy of the original green version. This booklet was the first printed version of the Toyota Way as defined by our mother company, TMC in Japan. As I read the booklet, I sensed a spiritual aspect of the Toyota Way, to which I quickly connected. It went beyond building cars, profits, quality, and other common topics for businesses. It focused on improving society, people, improvement, reflection, and the environment. I soon became a lifelong witness to the Toyota Way using any opportunity I could to evangelize it to others.

The first thing I learned from this booklet was that Toyota's principles were built upon two distinct pillars that supported each other: continuous improvement and respect for people. Together, these two pillars form what is known today as the *Toyota Way*. Prior to this experience, I heard about kaizen, kanban systems, and just-in-time (JIT) processing, as I had helped to set up the Ontario Parts Center (OPC) in 1993, which today is called the North American Parts Center California (NAPCC), located in Ontario, California. NAPCC is the embodiment of the Toyota Way and the TPS. Although I worked at NAPCC at its inception, I had not officially heard about Hoshin or the Toyota Way as a concept. The Toyota Way principles were all around me in that warehouse. I performed my job based on these principles, and lived the drive and dedication of these principles. They were a part of every operations planning document and every customer service document that I encountered. However, I was not formally introduced to the principles of the Toyota Way in those early years. Prior to the year 2001, at the Torrance, California, headquarters office, the NAPCC facility was built on the foundations of the TPS. I was connected to it very well, as I was responsible for making sure that the computer and radio frequency (RF) networks were running efficiently so that the parts could be moved throughout the warehouse to our customers JIT without *muda* (Japanese term for waste).

My lack of formal introduction to the Toyota Way principles is in no way a negative judgment on Toyota, but rather an indication of how Toyota's philosophies were taught in the early days in the U.S. sales divisions. For you see, although I worked at the NAPCC facility, I reported to the sales side of the company, as I supported information technology while reporting to human resources. In various parts of the sales division, the Toyota Way was implied in spirit and one just fell in line and became part of the culture (it was in our DNA!). There was not a lot of formal training being done on the sales side, as was the case on the warehouse side, on the manufacturing side, or in Japan. In fact, I was so engulfed in setting up and configuring the local area network (LAN), the wide area network (WAN), and the RF in the new warehouse that I never once realized I needed to take the time to learn the foundation to our company. And no one mandated that I do so. I guess you could say I just innately lived the spirit of the Toyota Way without realizing there was a bona fide, written Toyota Way philosophy until years later, in the office of this vice president.

I share this experience to point out that although Hoshin is the driver for all of Toyota's goals and objectives, many employees on the sales side did not understand it or embrace it. We simply lived it, and our divisional goals were shaped by it without us realizing it. Hoshin was more a part of our being rather than our conscious intellect.

TMC eventually began to mandate that the Toyota Way principles be incorporated into everything we did on the sales side. This mandate, albeit a push, was done gently with SMART goals. In fact, TMC suggested that the sales division look at how this could be done in a way that worked best for the division. It was at this time that I became intimately familiar with what is called the Toyota global content (Hoshin, TPS, Ji-Kotei-Kanketsu [JKK], Toyota Business Practice [TBP], and on the job development [OJD]) and began to explore how to help the sales division embrace the Toyota Way principles. I was not opposed to hard work, learning, and growing. While working in the University of Toyota, I was given a "sandbox" to experiment with to find innovative new ways to deliver training and transform hearts and minds. I did so by focusing on what I believed was the key to helping team members whole-heartedly embrace TPS, Hoshin, and other components of Toyota's global content. I believe that embracing these philosophies has a lot to do with the value that one places on concepts, objects, and people (Hartman, 1967), so I began to research the connection between value science, neuroscience, and Hoshin to inform my curiosity and exploration. The remainder of this introduction provides an overview of my discoveries.

People Side of Hoshin

As important as Hoshin Kanri is to implementing Lean management, there is more to successful Hoshin implementation than the tools and the strategic process. The success of Hoshin planning and implementation is solely dependent on the people who develop and implement it. Toyota leaders seem to understand the people side of Hoshin at the systemic level. However, I question whether they truly understood it at the intrinsic level of the individual. In other words, the entire process had to be understood, based on the valuation that a person placed on Hoshin, to the point where it had real meaning to the individual.

For example, Toyota values respect for people and diversity of thought and demonstrates this by providing benefits and compensation unlike any other company. So, when it came time to participate in the Hoshin process, the motivation for buy-in for those going through the process should have been based on a spirit of gratitude. Instead, monetary incentives were often not enough to drive the commitment needed for fully embracing Hoshin or the other global contents to take place. The missing piece existed because leaders were excellent at driving results and meeting month-end profits. However, they lacked the skills needed to manage projects and lead people, as Jim Lentz (the CEO) would constantly challenge the leaders to do. The people side of Hoshin is a more comprehensive look at the capacity of one's thinking and caring enough to help people improve and become the best that they can be, without feeling like they are being negatively judged. This mindset is needed if everyone is expected to embrace Hoshin Kanri.

Toyota did not invent the Hoshin Kanri process. However, Toyota successfully implements Hoshin Kanri and uses the tools in a way that many companies have been unable to replicate or emulate. This success has a lot to do with Toyota's focus on *quality thinking** and on something that Toyota calls *drive and dedication.*† Quality thinking is emphasized in Toyota's JKK, a tool training focused on creating documentation that a person can follow step-by-step as he or she performs work. It is also concerned with the thinking that is required to *build quality into the work process with ownership.*‡ More specifically, *Ji* means self or ownership, *Kotei* is the process, and *Kanketsu* is the completion of the final documentation or outputs.

JKK is mentioned here because it is a good example of where the people side of Hoshin can best be described. With JKK, there is an emphasis on ownership, not just the ownership of one's own work process, but owning a true concern for the customers by constantly thinking about them in each process along the way, since JKK is concerned with understanding who the customer is. For example, the customer is also the person responsible for the next step in the process. The JKK process requires documentation to be developed in such a way that error prevention and resolution is

---

* Derived from training taken at TMNA: a way of thinking that automatically builds quality into the process.

† Derived from training taken at TMNA: the way in which Toyota team members act toward customers and themselves.

‡ Derived from training taken at TMNA: this is about owning a problem through to the resolution.

built into the process and handled before the supervisor brings it up. This is an action that each Toyota employee is expected to perform, whether they work on the assembly line or in the office. For example, on the assembly line, one would pull the andon cord when a defect was noticed. In the office, a person would use his or her vocal cords. This is important because each action performed by an individual is *always* preceded by a decision (Hartman, 1967). In my opinion, quality thinking requires quality decisions, and quality decisions lead to quality actions. This is important because emotions play a critical role in one's ability to make decisions (Seymour & Dolan, 2008).

To understand how to obtain quality decisions, one must first understand the team member's decision pattern and what internally motivates that person to prioritize solutions to these quality decisions. In other words, there must first be a diagnosis of the person's capacity to make such decisions. Diagnosing and understanding one's decision patterns is not something that Toyota teaches. However, it is something that I have discovered is the missing link in the implementation of Toyota's overall global content (including Hoshin), and will certainly be the missing link when other companies attempt to implement Hoshin and LDM as well.

Value Science

In my quest to understand more about how people make quality decisions, I stumbled across the work of Robert S. Hartman. Hartman (1967) is considered the father of formal axiology (a scientific value theory). Axiology is a science that reveals how individuals think and make decisions. Hartman makes this information available to people by way of an assessment he calls the *Hartman Value Profile*™ (HVP). When this assessment is combined with the *Value Index*™ assessment and the *DISC*™ assessment, together they reveal not only how a person thinks and makes decisions, but also what motivates him or her to prioritize those decisions, and how those decisions are communicated to other people. Employees who are armed with this information about themselves are more self-aware and are more conscious of how they make decisions and communicate during the Hoshin process.

Bringing people together from different groups across the company and expecting them to negotiate goals and strategies for the next three to five years is synonymous with what happens during corporate merger integration. Two companies come together to improve their financial profits and competitiveness, not realizing that research shows that most mergers fail because they do not pay attention to the people side of the merger. It is estimated that companies are spending $2 trillion annually on merger acquisitions and between 70% and 90% of those acquisitions fail (Christensen et al., 2011). Many fail because of human resource–related issues (Napier, 1989). Several scientists, including Gilkey (1991), argue that "the high percentage of failure is mainly due to the fact that mergers and acquisitions are still designed with business and financial fit as primary conditions, leaving psychological and cultural issues as secondary concerns" (p. 33). Napier (1989) confirms that merger integrations fail because they do not appreciate and respect individuals in the process.

This is similar to what happens to individuals during the Hoshin journey when personalities clash. In healthcare, this can be even more catastrophic because lives are at stake. Understanding Hartman's work is the first step to understanding the people side of Hoshin Kanri. Hartman was nominated for a Nobel Peace Prize for his work on peace and his interest in good and evil. He was a German mathematician and judge who also earned two PhDs. Hartman applied mathematics to axiology, converting it from a philosophy to a science, and hence creating formal axiology, as we know it today.

Formal Axiology

Formal axiology has less to do with values as a noun (e.g., integrity and trust) and more to do with what people regard as valuable and the numerical value that one places on ideas, objects, and people. Hartman described this valuation as the *hierarchy of value*. The hierarchy of value consists of three main categories: systemic (S), extrinsic (E), and intrinsic (I). Each category is viewed from two different perspectives: (1) work-related worldview and (2) self worldview. Hoshin Kanri is typically taught, developed, and implemented systemically (i.e., as a concept or idea) and extrinsically (i.e., tangible) in the development of A3 documents, where most of the value is placed on the systemic and extrinsic. Rarely is it taught, developed, or implemented intrinsically (i.e., internally motivated by a person). It is this intrinsic valuation that is needed to drive the tools and strategies of the Hoshin process. Understanding the hierarchy of value provides an objective way to look at the people side of Hoshin and to understand how best to utilize its tools and strategies more productively and efficiently.

When Hartman turned axiology into a science, he discovered that the intrinsic carried a greater value than extrinsic, and the extrinsic carried a greater value than systemic (i.e., I > E > S). What this tells us is where we will obtain the greatest bang for our buck or, in the case of Hoshin, where we will gain the greatest value in the use of its tools and strategies. In other words, *the people side of Hoshin* has greater value than the *tools*, and the *tools* has a greater value than *Hoshin Kanri as a concept*. This does not mean that one does not care about Hoshin tools and strategy. It simply means that there needs to be a balance between the three (i.e., strategies, tools, and people) when developing and implementing Hoshin Kanri.

Three Areas of Hoshin Where Neuroscience Is Best Applied

As described in other chapters in this book, having a good mission and vision is critical to the Hoshin Kanri process. My experience at Toyota revealed that Toyota is not immune to the challenges that are presented during the development of Hoshin, even though we always had a good vision and mission, both of which drove the success of the company. As a midlevel manager, I did not participate in the creation of Hoshin at the TMC or executive level. However, I was often called on to develop conflict management workshops with executives and managers in other settings, which revealed the types of challenges that were faced in those early phases of the Hoshin process. Many would point to our consensus-building process and our inability to make timely decisions as the cause of delays in such strategies. However, I continue to believe that the challenge was not in the amount of time it took for us to decide, but rather in the capacity of the decision pattern of those who were responsible for those decisions and the communication challenges that were created during personal interactions.

In order for Hoshin to be developed, there is a need for the leader to make a choice to demonstrate unconditional positive regard for the Hoshin process and for others. Unconditional positive regard is a concept developed by the humanistic psychologist Carl Rogers. It is based on the notion that no matter what a person says or does, he or she is accepted and supported physically, mentally, emotionally, and verbally. Leaders also need to have good emotional intelligence (emotional quotient [EQ]) and understand how to avoid what is known as an *amygdala hijack*. Daniel Goleman coined *amygdala hijack* in his 1996 book titled *Emotional Intelligence*. It's a term used to describe the sudden onset of an emotional response, which occurs when our emotional memory takes over the emotions without logic or reason, and causes the body to go into a fight-or-flight mode, where the person displays strong negative emotions. Emotional intelligence has to do with individuals being able to understand their own emotions, as well as those of other people, and to label and discern between different feelings. This is important because emotions can become elevated during the Hoshin process. If this happens, respect and trust can be lost, thus creating a lose–lose situation and delaying the creation of Hoshin.

Workplace Direction

At Toyota, workplace direction has to do with identifying and understanding our customers and developing a mission and vision. This is where the strategic planning for Hoshin takes place. My understanding is that this is the phase of the process where ideas, feedback, and commitment are needed. However, if leaders approach this phase as a marketing event where they want to sell their own ideas or look good at the expense of others, this approach could easily derail Hoshin early on.

Several of my colleagues who share my vision to infuse neuroscience into the Toyota Way often collaborated with each other on our passion for the people side of Hoshin and other Toyota global content. We often imagined that one day we would utilize positive psychology, appreciative inquiry, narrative inquiry, transactional analysis, and other theories in the practical application of Toyota's global content. However, we were never able to get these ideas off the ground due to the timing of a 2014 Toyota headquarters relocation where several projects were put on hold or canceled. In my opinion, being able to include concepts from these tried-and-true theories ensures that employees will embrace the Toyota Way.

Hoshin Plan Development

In my experience at Toyota, I often wondered how my work contributed to Toyota's global vision. I understood the global vision; however, when the regional or functional visions were created, the ultimate goal and purpose often got lost in the words on the paper. Such was the case when the One Toyota move was announced on April 27, 2014. We received a set of cultural priorities that sounded great on paper (e.g., systemically); however, it was a little difficult to build strategies around it at the lower levels. So much emotional turmoil was being experienced because of the merger that no one had the opportunity to emotionally or cognitively connect the divisional Hoshin to the nicely written priorities.

Catch-Ball

The catch-ball process is the heart of the Hoshin plan development. The catch-ball process is also where the lack of EQ and the inability to recover from an amygdala hijack can create the greatest challenges. For it is in the catch-ball meetings where leaders are expected to collaborate with each other and share information that is intended to cascade to other divisions, departments, and individuals. Mutual purpose is important at this stage, and if leaders find themselves stuck in their emotions, team members will never learn how their work contributes to the bigger picture or learn how to carry out the work.

Neuroscience of Lean Management

NLM is a model that aligns to the concepts of TPS to bring awareness around how the components of TPS are understood through the lens of neuroscience. This information is a precursor to understanding Neuro-Hoshin, as it was derived from a comprehensive essay that I wrote while working through the dissertation process at Fielding Graduate University in Santa Barbara, California.

Lean production and Lean manufacturing originated from the philosophy of Japanese production systems. The focus with these systems is the elimination of muda (Japanese term for waste) and to reduce cost (Shingo & Dillon, 1989). Based on Taiichi Ohno's observations, Toyota created what are called the eight mudas: waiting, motion, rework, conveyance, overprocessing, inventory, overproduction, and unused human creativity. This is important because researchers are finding that the human capacity to process information is limited, causing individuals to compensate for this limitation by creating shortcuts that affect their judgments in decision making (Bazerman, 1998) and creating muda.

Most Lean literature focuses on the tool side of Lean, with some attention to teamwork as a key component of Lean production. The reason that companies who have attempted to implement Lean in non-Japanese cultures are finding it difficult to do so is because their focus has been on the tools. But Lean also has a human side, for example, mentoring to develop Lean thinking.

Lean thinking is primarily focused on value. Value is the thread that connects various versions of Lean concepts. In 1996, Womack and Jones posited that value is considered the first principle of Lean thinking because it is focused on reducing cost and eliminating waste on the shop floor on behalf of the customer (Womack & Jones, 1996). When thinking about Lean concepts, it is easy to focus on the tools; however, tools only make up about 20% of the Lean efforts. The other 80% consists of the practices and behaviors of the people who lead these efforts (Mann, 2009).

Lean leadership is looked upon as the foundation, which determines the success of a Lean initiative. Senior leaders are responsible for paving the way for the 80% of practices and behaviors to be successfully accomplished (Mann, 2009). Mann (2009) referred to this leadership as the missing link in Lean management because it was responsible for shaping the culture that would allow Lean processes to be successful. The human side of Lean can be expanded far beyond just mentoring to develop Lean thinking. The human side also reaches into a way of experiencing leadership that has the potential of taking Lean management to the next level of understanding.

Brain science has been advancing so much that scientists now have the conditions and equipment to understand how different parts of the brain function and how neuropathways affect the way people respond and behave (Schwartz-Hebron, 2012). This information can now be applied to management systems in a practical way, as seen in the way in which this book applies both neuroscience and Lean management to the NLM in the next section.

New Body of Knowledge: Neuroscience of Lean Management

Researchers who have attempted to look at neuroscience and Lean management have done so by exploring connections between quality management and brain functioning (Lagrosen & Travis, 2015). For example, Lagrosen and Travis (2015) compared Peter Deming's four systems of profound knowledge—appreciation for a system, knowledge about variation, theory of knowledge, and psychology (Deming, 1994/2000)—with the five principles of brain function in neuroscience: coherence, homeostatic feedback loops, neural plasticity, brain areas underlying emotions, and cognition contributing to decision making.

Holzak and Olsen (2014) discussed the psychological factors behind the philosophies, principles, and practices of Lean using the best-selling book

Thinking, Fast and Slow (2011) by Nobel Prize winner Daniel Kahnerman. Kahnerman (2011) made a distinction between fast and slow thinking with a metaphor he called System 1 and System 2. System 1 is the core of associative memory, which interprets what's going on in the world in an instant, intuitively. System 2 thinking is a more controlled, statistical way of thinking, which takes more time (Kahnerman, 2011, pp. 13–14). In their article, Hozak and Olsen (2015) were concerned with analyzing how Lean utilizes System 1 and System 2 thinking as described by Kahnerman. Hozak and Olsen (2014) posited that the beneficial bias created by Lean thinking, for example, framing, priming, anchoring, and halo effects, takes advantage of System 1's fast thinking, while Lean work practices encourage employee involvement, data-driven decision making, and carefully defined processes, which take advantage of System 2 thinking.

To understand the impact that neuroscience has on the elimination of waste and the reduction of cost within Lean management, it's important to understand the eight mudas of overproduction, delay, transport, processing, inventory, wasted motions, the waste of making defective products, and unused human creativity (Shingo & Dillon, 1989, p. 191). All the mudas require a lot of planning and focus to be able to see and eliminate the waste, which means they stimulate the frontal lobe.

The error-checking mechanism of the brain appears to be triggered in situations of waiting and having to correct defects. Transportation and inventory involve compassion, because these two mudas are most responsible for creating situations where the customer is not able to receive the products either because they got broken during transportation or are not available in inventory. The ability to adopt a noncost perspective and allow the customer to drive the demand and price is key. Overprocessing, overproduction, and defects can all stimulate the area of the brain that creates a sense of frustration and taps into the primitive area of the brain that could stimulate a fight-or-flight sensation when trying to deliver the right product at the right time in the right quantity. Being able to manage one's emotions, self-regulate one's thinking, and activate a more positive set of emotions is essential within LDM, as well as within Hoshin Kanri. Table 0.1 compares neuroscience brain activation to the foundation of TPS and indicates how the muda of LDM aligns to neuroscience and brain structure.

Table 0.1 Neuroscience of Lean Management: Comparative Analysis between Organizational Neuroscience and Lean Management (TPS)

Neuroscience	Frontal Lobe	Parietal Lobe	Anterior Cingulate	Limbic System
	Activated when focusing, planning, reasoning, reading, or speaking. ⟺	Gives a sense of separation from other people and things in the world. ⟺	Activated when empathy and compassion for others surface. ⟺	Primitive area of the brain; holds negative emotion. ⟺
Toyota Production System mudas	The focus of TPS is the elimination of waste and the reduction of cost (Shingo & Dillon, 1989, p. 95). This requires lots of planning and focus.	The worker–machine relationship is important in TPS and has been separated for efficiency (Shingo & Dillon, 1989).	Adopting a noncost principle where customers drive the price, not profit, shows compassion for the customer (Shingo & Dillon, 1989, p. 75).	Delivering right production, at the right time and in the right quantity deep meaning (Shingo & Dillon, 1989, p. 69). A positive attitude is key to eliminating waste (p. 80).
Areas Were Neuroscience and TPS Merge				
Transportation	√		√	–
Inventory	√		√	–
Motion	√			–
Waiting	√	√		
Overprocessing	√			√
Overproduction	√	√		√
Defects	√	√		√

Neuro-Hoshin

Neuro-Hoshin is a simple concept by which value science and neuroscience are used to understand what is going on inside one's thinking when something like a Hoshin plan is being developed and implemented during catch-ball meetings. The goal of Neuro-Hoshin is to use this information to help individuals understand what may be emotionally and cognitively blocking them from developing and implementing Hoshin. What I am about to share is focused on the thinking part of neuroscience, which I call *value cognition*. This concept, which is the main component of Neuro-Hoshin, occurs in the prefrontal cortex of the brain. As part of the decision-making process during a catch-ball meeting, each participant in the meeting unconsciously asks two questions about rules, results, and other people:

1. How clearly do the leaders understand how their Hoshin-driven decisions will impact the rules that the company expects them to follow, the results they are expected to achieve, and how these decisions will be accepted by other people in the organization?
2. How important will all this be to the leaders?

From a decision-making perspective, the capacity by which leaders value rules (systemic valuation), results (extrinsic valuation), and other people (intrinsic valuation) will determine how effective they will be at strategic planning. The order in which this decision process occurs determines an individual's thinking pattern (e.g., rules, results, other people; results, other people, rules; other people, results, rules; etc.). Hartman calls these components the workplace view. Overvaluation or undervaluation of the rules, results, and other people will cause a person to respond in a catch-ball meeting in ways that are misunderstood by others, especially when there are representatives of varying degrees of clarity in the catch-ball meeting all competing for what they feel is right. In other words, some people may overvalue or undervalue these components because of their level of clarity of the rules, results, or other people (Table 0.2). For example, the participants in a catch-ball meeting may have *transition* clarity (i.e., they don't understand the topic at all), *visible* clarity (i.e., they have very little understanding of the topic), unconventional clarity (i.e., they have creative understanding of the topic), *good* clarity (i.e., they understand the topic well), or *excellent* clarity (i.e., they have crystal-clear understanding of the topic). The clarity scores

Table 0.2 Hierarchy of Value

	Systemic	*Extrinsic*	*Intrinsic*
Work view	Rules	Results	Other people
Self-view	Self-direction	Role awareness	Self-esteem

Note: Robert S. Hartman is the original author. Wayne Carpenter (with Axiometrics) and Greg Smith (with Maui Analysis) provided more practical labeling and descriptions.

provide powerful insights into understanding the consequences of decisions, or how decisions will impact the rules, results, or other people.

An extreme overvaluation of the rules may cause individuals to think that the rules are written in stone and should never be broken, even in a brainstorming session pertaining to company goals. On the other hand, an undervaluation of the rules could cause the individuals to be viewed as rebels who want to do things their own way and feel that rules are guidelines for other people, not themselves. In the case of results, individuals who overvalue them are going to be doers. In catch-ball meetings, they will insist on taking actions now to get results without achieving any kind of consensus. Individuals who cannot see the consequences of accomplishing results and do not value results may be extremely hesitant and cautious in making decisions and could derail the meeting or make incorrect decisions.

Participants in catch-ball meetings who overvalue people may be overly agreeable, feeling that the other people in the meeting can do no wrong. On the contrary, participants who undervalue people will assume the worst about the other people in the catch-ball meeting, appear pessimistic, not trust what is being discussed, and play defense with any idea that is presented. The key in all these examples is balance. The idea is to help leaders become self-aware of their decision patterns and teach them to balance their decisions more purposefully.

The workplace view (Table 0.2) is just half the battle that can influence the outcome of a catch-ball meeting. There is also the aspect of the self-view, which Hartman divides into three components: (1) self-esteem, (2) role awareness, and (3) future direction—all of which can themselves be overvalued or undervalued, impacting Hoshin discussed in the catch-ball meeting.

People with low self-esteem may not trust their decisions in these meetings and feel they cannot get anything right. They usually have a perception that they should be perfect in these meetings and feel defeated when

Table 0.3 Levels of Clarity

Ranking	Type	Description
Highest (5)	Excellent clarity	Has crystal clear understanding and clarity
4	Good clarity	Has good understanding and clarity
3	Unconventional clarity	Has out-of-the-box creative understanding and clarity
2	Visible clarity	Understands some things and does not understand other things
Lowest (1)	Transition clarity	Does not understand the situation at all

Note: Robert S. Hartman is the original author. Wayne Carpenter (with Axiometrics) and Greg Smith (with Maui Analysis) provided more practical labeling and descriptions.

they are not. On the other hand, people who overvalue themselves in these meetings might feel that they are "God's gift to the world"; their ideas are the best ideas, and they are perfect. People who overvalue their jobs may appear like workaholics who refuse to give up in the meeting and may want to work all night at getting things right. On the other hand, people who hate their jobs will feel that the catch-ball session is a waste of time and that they don't know where the meeting is going anyway, so either they check out or their behavior is more passive-aggressive during the journey.

Finally, people who overvalue their future will feel that they can see exactly where they need to be. If the catch-ball session is not going in that same direction, they may push back and become frustrated. On the other hand, some people feel that their future is dark and disquieting and the catch-ball process is not going to make it better. These folks will most likely sound like doubting Thomases and not provide input or cooperation. Again, Hartman was able to measure one's thinking and apply the same level of clarity (Table 0.3) to this self-view as he did to the worldview.

Applying Value Science and Neuroscience to LDM and Neuro-Hoshin

NLM and Neuro-Hoshin are two concepts that can be used to provide self-awareness to leaders and staff who have the responsibility of implementing Hoshin Kanri in the workplace. It can be achieved by adding these concepts to the Hoshin refresher classes or by providing one-on-one coaching to leaders using their customized results from the HVP assessment.

Why Are Value Science and Neuroscience Important to the Hoshin Journey?

Hoshin planning initiates the LDM process. Hoshin planning enables continuous improvement and continuous learning. The challenge that many people have with continuous improvement is understanding how to make the necessary changes to initiate continuous improvement. Whether it's letting go of unwanted behaviors and habits, negotiating with others in a catch-ball meeting, forgiving someone who hurt them, or letting go of the fear that Deming describes in TQM no. 8, the antidote is change. The brain plays a role in change through a physiological process called neuroplasticity. Neuroplasticity is the mind's ability to change the brain. In other words, when you change your mind, you change your brain. Understanding this concepts places personal power for one's behavior back into the hands of the individual, allowing the individual to rewire their brain by changing how they think (Schwartz & Beyette, 1997). NLM and Neuro-Hoshin bring awareness into the catch-ball process and allow each participant the opportunity to shift their mindset, by asking two important questions:

1. How clearly do I understand?
2. How important is it to me?

Asking these two questions stimulates blood flow to the prefrontal cortex of the brain and away from the amygdala, where negative emotions reside. In doing so, a person can organize, think, and focus more clearly on the decisions and actions needed to successfully implement any catch-ball activity. From a value science perspective, these questions help individuals realize, in a catch-ball meeting, the very moment when they are experiencing an amygdala hijack, that there is a cost to the consequences of how they are communicating or behaving, whether positively or negatively, and allow them an opportunity to consciously choose to communicate or behave differently. For example, it could be costing them their effectiveness, or their happiness, or their relationship with their peers or their company, or it could cause them to create a bad Hoshin. Neuro-Hoshin will help an individual make different choices, different value judgments, and more effective decisions. It all goes back to their perceptions of value and how it is applied during the catch-ball process.

Hartman posits says that "we will be calling anything good that fulfills its meaning and bad anything that does not ... though the measure of value is universal and objective." The thing to remember here is that although the measure of value is objective, the application of it by the human brain is subjective. Because the brain is never objective. This implies that the hierarchy of value exists, is objective, and is universally true and applicable, like gravity. So, whenever a person's subjective mind violates an objective science, like the hierarchy of value in a catch-ball meeting, the consequences will be seen immediately and will get progressively worse if not resolved. Knowing that the human brain, and the mind that resides within it, is never objective brings the kind of awareness to a leadership team that allows them to throw ideas around that are in line with objective value science, creating a win–win situation that has a much better chance of being implemented by those who understand the value Hoshin brings to them personally.

In conclusion, I am eternally grateful to Toyota for allowing me the opportunity to research and test out new ideas. I am in love with Toyota and what the company stands for. Many Toyota employees would agree that they feel a sense of security when working for this company. Even though I was not introduced to the Toyota Way until 2001, I was still fortunate to eventually become a certified trainer for the TBP conducted by TMC. I am also a certified JKK trainer and have received several trainings on Toyota's version of Hoshin Kanri. I'm honored to have had this experience and feel blessed to be able to share my testimony and research with others.

References

Bazerman, M. (1998). *Judgment in Managerial Decision-Making* (4th ed.). New York: Wiley & Sons.

Christensen, C. M., Alton, R., Rising, C., & Waldeck, A. (2011, March). The big idea: The new M&A playbook. *Harvard Business Review*.

Deming, W. E. (1994/2000). *The New Economics for Industry, Government, Education*. Cambridge, MA: MIT Press.

Gilkey, R. T. (1995). The psychodynamics of upheaval: Intervening in merger and acquisitions. In Kets de Vries, M. F. B. (Ed.), *Organization on the Couch*. San Francisco: Jossey-Bass.

Hartman, R., & Ellis, A. R. (2013). *Freedom to Live: The Robert Hartman Story*. Eugene, OR: Wipf & Stock.

Hartman, R. S. (1967). *The Structure of Value; Foundations of Scientific Axiology*. Carbondale, IL: Southern Illinois University Press.

Hozak, K., & Olsen, E. O. (2015). Lean psychology and the theories of "Thinking, Fast and Slow." *International Journal of Lean Six Sigma*, 6(3), 206–225. doi: 10.1108/IJLSS-10-2014-0030.

Kahneman, D. (2011). *Thinking, Fast and Slow*. New York: Farrar, Straus and Giroux.

Lagrosen, Y., & Travis, F. T. (2015). Exploring the connection between quality management and brain functioning. *TQM Journal, 27*(5), 565–575. doi: 10.1108/TQM-08-2013-0093.

Mann, D. (2009). The missing link: Lean leadership. *Frontiers of Health Services Management, 26*(1), 15–26.

Napier, N. (1989). Mergers and acquisitions, human-resource issues and outcomes: A review and suggested typology. *Journal of Management Studies, 26*(3), 271–289. doi: 10.1111/j.1467-6486.1989.tb00728.x.

Schwartz-Hebron, R. (2012). Using neuroscience to effect change in the workplace. *Employment Relations Today, 39*(2), 11–15. doi: 10.1002/ert.21360.

Schwartz, J. M., & Beyette, B. (1997). *Brain Lock*. New York: Regan.

Seymour, B., & Dolan, R. (2008). Emotion, decision making, and the amygdala. *Neuron, 58*(5), 662–671. doi: 10.1016/j.neuron.2008.05.020.

Shingo, S., & Dillon, A. P. (1989). *A Study of the Toyota Production System from an Industrial Engineering Viewpoint*. Cambridge, MA: Productivity Press.

Womack, J., & Jones, D. T. (1996). *Lean Thinking: Banish Waste and Create Wealth for Your Corporation*. New York: Simon & Schuster.

Chapter 1

Hoshin and Lean Daily Management

With Hoshin planning and Lean daily management (LDM) in place and actively being deployed, your organization goes from passively playing defense to playing offense, building for the future by having the skills, infrastructure, and culture to get there. Your staff will know the *why* behind the *what*, and the leadership rounds and leader daily disciplines will add discipline and accountability that keep focus on those critical goals throughout the year. Also, the translation of the Hoshin planning goals to the LDM board will add the *why* behind the *what* to the focus of the LDM boards, what processes and issues are being looked at, the rationale behind the numerical goals, and other factors as well.

The "Lean journey" that any organization undertakes is a journey in every sense of the word. It starts off with a few tentative steps, never knowing exactly what the next turn in the road will unveil, or what the response or repercussions will be. Also, you have never been to the ultimate destination, so it is difficult to know where you are truly going. Therefore, it is critical to have a "sensei" (or expert, guide, or mentor) to help guide your journey. One of the many purposes of this book is to serve part of this purpose as your sensei! Practitioners who have spent their career practicing Lean and "making the mistakes for you" allow you to "borrow their learning curve" and thus not have to make all the same mistakes. Part of this understanding of the Lean journey is that there is truly no final destination when you "are finally there"—that is the "continuous" part of continuous improvement! The journey is truly more important than the destination, as the disciplined journey is what changes the DNA of your organization, drives a culture of change, develops your people and teams into problem solvers, and fundamentally changes the roles and effectiveness of your leaders and managers—for the better!

You may be aware of the LDM approach, which is a fundamentally different way of engaging teams in problem solving outside of formal Lean projects. That is, rather than Lean being driven by a system of facilitator-driven projects that are potentially widely dispersed and rare for any individual in an organization, a system is set up and teams are developed to have problem solving done daily (during brief 10- to 15-minute meetings) throughout the organizations. Leaders round on multiple levels in their span of control to (1) be aware of what is going on, (2) provide guidance where appropriate to the team, and most importantly, (3) take action items that require their leadership, authority, or span of control. Through this approach, the fundamental role of a leader is changed and the "cadence" of a leader's day shifts to supporting and enabling problem solving throughout their span of control, rather than just sitting at their desk or in meetings and interfacing with staff rarely and primarily through e-mail. If you aren't familiar with this approach, which is complementary and supports a successful Hoshin initiative, *Lean Daily Management for Healthcare Field Book* (Productivity Press, 2016) is very helpful. Another useful resource is the article "Big Hospital Improvements Start Small: Lean Daily Management Helped Make a Texas Medical Center's Lean Six Sigma Program Effective" (http://www.iise.org/uploadedFiles/IIE /Author_permissions/ISESept16Berlanga.pdf). (This article is provided with permission of the Institute of Industrial and Systems Engineers from the September 2016 issue of *ISE*, Copyright © 2016 Institute of Industrial and Systems Engineers. All rights reserved.)

As we begin our Lean journey, and throughout our continuous journey, it is critical to periodically take a step back and ask, "Why are we doing this?" Part of the answer to this question is that we are trying to solve problems, eliminate waste, develop our people, improve flow, and add value to the customer. If we take one more step back and look at an even higher perspective, we are trying to strengthen our overall organization and develop a system that will help us dynamically and effectively achieve our organization's goals, provide long-term stable employment for the individuals and teams we are employing, and provide value to our patients and the community and society as a whole. If you think back to the Toyota house model, it has a clearly and undeniably strong focus on people.

If we focus exclusively on solving problems, eliminating waste, and improving flow without an overall objective or guiding vision, then we are in danger of "popcorn kaizen" and improving efficiencies without necessarily linking these improvements to the bottom line or creating a unified patient experience or overall organization vision. This could also be looked at as the difference between tactics and strategy—without linking all the tactics together to move toward the strategy, we are in danger of winning the battle but losing the war.

Fortunately, the Lean tool kit has a powerful, effective, and disciplined way of achieving this, but it requires persistence and diligence to be successful. When linking Hoshin planning with LDM, these two approaches are mutually supportive and beneficial, which will be explained further in the following sections. The critical concept to understand is that the strategy and vision of the organization needs to be linked from the top level of the organization down to the front lines, with detailed and thoughtful translation and buy-in at all levels.

When this is done properly, these translated and negotiated goals and objectives can be directly transferred to the structure and function of the LDM boards that have been previously explored. The LDM boards then become the *how* to much of the *what* that was identified through the Hoshin planning process, and they become a tangible and visible way for leaders at all levels to physically and visually assess the strength of the linkages and progress of the teams toward these goals. This is an example of LDM boards being used to assess the effectiveness and strength of strategy deployment in an organization.

Hoshin planning is, at its most basic level, cascaded, negotiated, translated, and quantified goals that begin at the top of the organization (mission, vision, values, strategy, and goals) and on through to the front lines. When done properly, there is "line of sight" for all members of an organization that provides relevance and meaning for their improvement efforts and daily tasks. If done properly, anyone in the organization who has been involved in the process can explain how focusing on improving a specific activity or task contributes to the overall goals or objectives of the organization.

An example of this from a historical perspective was when President John F. Kennedy visited Cape Canaveral and asked a janitor what his job was. The janitor responded that he was helping to put a man on the moon! A parallel example for healthcare would be to ask the same question of a housekeeper working in the operating room, and instead of them saying that they cleaned rooms, they would respond, "I am on the front line of infection control and improving patient outcomes." Through their focus on improving the room turnover and cleaning process and adherence to best practices, they would see themselves as literally helping to save lives! In addition to Hoshin planning helping to achieve organizational goals and objectives, it provides significant relevance to the daily tasks that staff do.

Rather than just "doing work," they are contributing to something "greater" and have relevance and significance beyond just the superficial interpretation of their daily work.

To get to this level of significance, relevance, and meaning is not easy, but it is well worth the journey. Some of you may be thinking, "We already do goal setting and we have this taken care of." If you are so confident in this, we recommend that you take a second look! A great way to do this is to go to the front line of your organization and ask them what they are doing and, most importantly, why. If they respond with "That is my job" or "My boss told me to do it" or "That is what we have always done," it is clearly a sign of a disconnect. If they can tie it to a greater significance, to the customer or society, then it is strong validation of a higher level of alignment and meaning. When asking them these questions, it is critical not to "lead" them, as their response must be direct and honest, not out of fear, coercion, or rehearsed or forced.

Most organizations do annual goal setting, but it is essentially done *to* your employees and organization, with a very top-down "deployment" approach that leaves staff feeling that the goals are just words on a page with little or no meaning. The industry standard approach that often is described by this top-down approach is management by objectives (MBO). Most of us have personally experienced this; the authors definitely have. We have sat down with our boss and set goals for ourselves (such as personal development) and had goals handed down to us (to decrease cost, increase sales, etc.) and then went back to our normal jobs for the next year. At our annual review, our boss takes out our goals, and neither they nor we have looked at them during the intervening year. Your review is essentially dependent on whether your boss likes you. The goal setting was a fundamentally useless exercise and didn't drive any action, problem solving, or prioritization over the entire year. You just "did your job" and reacted to what happened on a daily basis and/or the inconsistent direction by management, depending on the quarterly financials. In essence, it was rather haphazard and primarily focused on reaction and "firefighting." With such a system (or a lack thereof), it is no wonder that many executives wonder why their organizations aren't progressing toward their goals or achieving what is needed to prosper and grow. With this sort of broken system persisting for many years, eventually the organizational dysfunction and lack of direction have accumulated enough waste and inefficiency that staffing cuts are necessary to stay profitable or survive.

As these cuts take place, morale plummets, our best staff leave for more promising organizations, and a "death spiral" often persists for years to come—not a desirable path to take! Hoshin planning provides a much more desirable path to take, but it takes commitment, patience, discipline, and focus to realize these critical results and organizational paradigm changes!

Chapter 2

Strategy Deployment in Healthcare 101

To effectively deploy and integrate Hoshin planning into your organization, there are a significant number of detailed aspects that must be put into place for it to be effective, which will be covered in the following sections. Don't be overwhelmed with thinking that all these pieces need to be put into place right away! As with most aspects of building a holistic Lean system, it requires a long-term perspective, trial and error, refinement of terminology, and integration with technical *and* social systems. These different aspects require discipline, reinforcement, oversight, and empowering staff—which are often an organizational and cultural challenge that must be overcome in time.

Setting SMART Goals

The SMART goal framework is very effective for helping to educate staff on setting effective and meaningful goals, and avoiding many of the common pitfalls that result in meaningless, unaligned, and ineffective goals. We will go through these one at a time to better understand what they are and why they are important.

- *Specific*: Goals should be clearly written and straightforward, and define what you are going to do. An effective way to evaluate this qualitatively is in how briefly and concisely the goal is written. Often a long series of statements and adjectives is a sign that the goal is ambiguous and not well defined. Just like with an A3 problem statement, a short, clear, and concise goal statement is a sign that a significant amount of thought and "distillation" has been done to get to the core, specific goal.

■ *Measurable*: A goal should have some objective way to evaluate whether it has been achieved, or if progress has been made toward the goal. This is a challenging aspect of goal setting that often becomes a stumbling block, especially in healthcare. When goals are set that say things like "increase," "decrease," or "improve," if there is not a current baseline measure, then these goal terms are meaningless. How can we improve if we don't know where we are now or how to measure? If we improve the process and can only say, "It feels better!" or "We know it is better," these are not strong validations of improvement. Another phrase that reflects this is, "We can't improve what we can't measure!" Improvement is also based on experimentation, and without some form of measurement, we can't do experiments and evaluate the effectiveness of our countermeasures. At the same time, many processes in healthcare don't have readily available (or meaningful) data, and this can be a stumbling block for staff setting goals. They sometimes feel like they need perfect or highly defensible data—just like problem solving, often "back of the envelope" data that roughly approximates process performance is sufficient and a huge improvement from where we started!

■ *Achievable*: Goals need to "thread a needle" between challenging us to improve and being achievable—having the leader and team believe that they are achievable. If we set an overly aggressive goal, then the team feels oppressed by it and doesn't believe that it can actually be accomplished, and it has the opposite effect of motivation. In essence, it leaves the teams de-motivated! If it is too easy to achieve, it is not driving improvement, and it is an exercise in futility (actually a waste). Therefore, it needs to achieve what Toyota calls a "productive level of stress"— enough pressure and focus to improve, but not too much or too little, both of which result in little or no improvement. This delicate balance is challenging to achieve and takes practice, homework, and discipline, but it pays off handsomely for the staff and organization as a whole.

■ *Results focused*: Goals should measure improvement or outcomes, not tasks or activities. It is common to see tasks listed as goals, such as "implement" or "complete," which are often loosely (at best!) tied to some improvement focus. In a Lean daily management (LDM) system, this is essentially like skipping "diagnosis" and "symptom" on a huddle board and jumping straight to "treatment plan." By doing this, we are not setting ourselves up for "experimenting," which is absolutely critical to both goal setting and LDM. Our treatment plan is the experiment to improve something. If we are doing an experiment without linking it closely to something measurable that we are trying to improve, then there is no feedback loop. We are just "guessing" with tasks that may or may not be improving what we want to improve. We may very well be implementing changes that add cost and complexity, and may not be improving anything, and this would mean that our goals are actually working against the organization—which we absolutely don't want!

- *Time-bound*: Goals need to be clearly tied to a timeline for implementation, incremental goal attainment, and allowing for uncertainty of the effectiveness of the tasks or countermeasures identified to achieve the goal. If there is no clear timeline tied to the goal, then working toward it is likely to be procrastinated until close to the end of a specified time period, with daily operational demands getting in the way. If we spread out the timeline over the entire year, we are assuming that everything will go exactly as planned, which rarely occurs in most organizations (or in our personal or family life!). Therefore, we should set a more aggressive (but achievable) timeline with more frequent and short-term intermediary goals to achieve the goal earlier than otherwise necessary. This is (reasonably) assuming that not everything will go as planned, which will allow us time to do problem solving and identify new or modified countermeasures to try (plan–do–check–act [PDCA]) to figure out a new path to achieving the goal. Include in this timeline regular meetings with your manager or supervisor, as this will help hold yourself (or your direct report) accountable, and results in the normal human behavior of increasing the intensity (and progress) of work toward a goal before a "tollgate" meeting.

Now that we have covered the basic SMART goal framework, we will go into more detail on a few related aspects to emphasize critical aspects of goal setting and alignment.

Setting Goals to "Strive for," Not Tasks!

Our goals should be something to strive for, which means there is uncertainty to how we will achieve it (this is good!). Lexus (Toyota's luxury brand) has arguably the best statement that epitomizes this concept: "the relentless pursuit of perfection." The concept of striving and relentlessly striving toward something is absolutely critical to Hoshin planning and continuous improvement in general. Part of this is the fact that we live in a very dynamic and ever-changing world. Theoretically, if the world was static and didn't change, we could achieve perfection with enough time and focus.

Fortunately (or unfortunately, depending on how you look at it), the world is ever changing, as are the environment, regulation, competition, market, staff, leadership, and other factors, so continuously improving is essential to even maintain the status quo. Therefore, setting goals to strive for instead of tasks to accomplish aligns very closely with continuous improvement, problem solving, and LDM.

Therefore, if we focus on tasks alone, we may complete all these and accomplish nothing. A medical example would be a surgeon doing all the correct steps and still having the patient die or the surgery not resulting in the desired outcome. Even if we can objectively say that we did the prescribed steps, if the desired outcome didn't come to fruition, then we need to reflect (Hansei) and evaluate our inherent assumptions and the steps that we took. This is just like "jumping to the right-hand side" of an A3! A worse case (and common outcome) is that we invest resources or add process steps or work that doesn't eliminate waste or improve the process, and actually adds steps, expends resources, and/or adds complexity. This means that we would have been better off doing nothing at all than doing what we did—the opposite of Lean or Toyota Production System (TPS) thinking!

If we focus on setting goals to strive for, and identify tasks that we think will help (address the root causes), this is a much more effective way to get better. We focus our efforts on gathering data to identify the "gap" between where we are and where we want to be, on identifying the root causes, and then sequentially experiment with trying different countermeasures to move closer to this goal. With this approach, we have set up an environment of A3 thinking and experimentation and iterative PDCA problem solving to move us toward our goal in a purposeful, effective, flexible, and high-impact way, that is, as long as we "trust the process."

Alignment or Translation (Why and What)

At this point, it is critical that we take a step back from the goals that we are working on and ask more fundamental questions: (1) Are our goals aligned and meaningful in terms of moving the organization toward its overall goals, and (2) are these goals further translated to each level of the organization so that they are measurable and meaningful (and SMART)? If not, then setting goals that are only SMART and not aligned or translated will just result in haphazard, disconnected, and often meaningless work that results in little or no organizational progression toward our strategy and goals. Therefore, SMART goals that aren't aligned and translated are anything but "smart" goals!

Organizations commonly set strategic or long-term goals and vision but don't translate these in a meaningful way throughout the organization all the way to the front line. If you ask most senior leaders what the organizational strategy is, they can usually tell you many or all of them. If you ask a midlevel manager or director what these are (or ask any detail), your success rate drops dramatically—especially if you ask them how they can personally impact these on a daily basis! If you continue farther down through the organization and eventually get to frontline supervisors and frontline staff, they are very unlikely to know what these strategies and long-term goals are, and even less likely to know how they can impact these on a daily basis. You usually get a "deer in the headlights" look from these staff, which is the most powerful argument for the critical need for Hoshin planning in an organization! If an organization sets lofty goals and an aggressive strategy to realize these goals but doesn't do the translation or have staff set SMART goals, then it is essentially setting itself up for failure! From a numerical perspective, you are setting ambitious goals but excluding 99% of your organization's staff from truly participating in the process or contributing to the achievement of these goals. That leaves *a lot* of responsibility on the remaining 1%, which is essentially an unwinnable situation (which is why most organizations are not successful at the medium- and long-term achievement of their strategic goals).

Without investing the time or effort to align and translate these goals, they are hoping that they manifest themselves in actionable behavior throughout the year, which is a recipe for failure! Another way to describe this is the phrase "Hope is not a plan!" One of the fundamental Lean wastes is not utilizing the creativity and problem solving of our staff, and if we (through inaction) don't utilize the creativity and problem solving of our staff throughout our organization to move toward achieving our strategy, goals, and long-term plan, then this is a systemic and chronic manifestation of this fundamental waste! Given that healthcare is even more biased toward staff (as opposed to equipment and other forms of cost or capital) in terms of staffing cost representing that vast majority of expenses on an ongoing basis, the magnitude of this waste is even more severe than in some other industries.

Every person in the organization needs to have goals translated in a meaningful way so that they can know how their work and daily activities help support organizational goals. Without this translation to meaningful, SMART, countable goals, they serve almost no purpose and can even be counterproductive in many respects. When goals are effectively translated throughout an organization, and linked to LDM (which we will talk about more later), then the impact can be profound and powerful! Leaders can walk through an organization, from the top board to the frontline boards (and every level in between) and see how the strategic goals of the organization have been effectively translated and are being actively implemented (active problem solving and experimentation). Also, leaders can round and assess the health of their strategy deployment. For example, where are goals actively progressing and being worked on and where are they not? This provides a highly effective "early warning system" for leaders (maybe a sketch of an early warning system for leaders on strategy) that are actively engaged in this way—rather than waiting until the end of the year when it usually becomes evident that goals or strategy are not proving effective or impacting the organization in the intended way, when it is too late to do anything about it! When leaders regularly do this, they are able to do "course corrections" midyear and actually have a meaningful impact on goal attainment throughout the year.

This early warning system is also highly effective at helping to compensate for a shift that has been happening in healthcare for several decades, which consists of the "flattening" of the organizational structure and the accompanying reduction in management "bandwidth." Span of control and having some extra capacity for leadership engagement, problem solving, support, and staff development is a critical aspect of Toyota's organizational structure, and aspects of this have been "withering" in healthcare for decades. To control cost, frontline supervisors, leads, and other levels of midlevel management have been disappearing, sometimes resulting in a supervisor or director having up to (literally) 150 direct reports! With this dilution of management, and the accompanying number of "fires to fight," the pressures on midlevel and senior managers have increased significantly, so it is even more critical for them to be able to make effective use of their time in a way that is meaningful and impactful to the organization (rather than just monitoring budgets, dealing with human resources issues, and fighting fires). By having the managers round on these boards, they can "zero in" on the major gaps and where they can have the biggest impact as managers to help encourage, support, and break down barriers for their teams, and not expend energy trying to help teams that are already making great progress. This system allows our leaders to really make the best use of their time and focus their energies, which is absolutely critical in the modern healthcare environment or hospital.

To illustrate what a Hoshin-like translation of goals would look like (in terms of a personal frontline staff connection of a high-level goal to their daily tasks), we will look at one of the most audacious goals that has ever been set:

> I believe that this nation should commit itself to achieving the goal, before this decade is out, of landing a man on the moon and returning him safely to the earth. No single space project in this period will be more impressive to mankind, or more important for the long-range exploration of space.

> **President John F. Kennedy**
> *Address to Congress on Urgent National Needs, May 25, 1961*

This was one of the most ambitious goals that has ever been articulated, and set in motion a tremendous investment in research, time, energy, resources, and national pride. Beyond the obvious technical and other aspects of goal, one would wonder what a frontline staff member not focused on the core technical work would see as their role?

When President Kennedy visited the Space Center in Cape Canaveral, Florida, he asked a janitorial staff member what his job was, expecting a very normal response, such as "I clean the floors or I take out the garbage." The janitor responded, "I am helping to put a man on the moon!" This is a historical example of a high-level strategic or long-term goal being translated (culturally) to a frontline staff member, who helped elevate the staff member's thinking beyond just viewing their seemingly mundane tasks, and instead linking them to the high-level goal: putting a man on the moon. A fundamental tenant of the TPS is respect for people, and appreciating the significance and contribution of the seemingly mundane tasks and activities of staff in a greater context is a great example of the potential power of the translation and alignment of goals. With each staff member seeing the greater significance of their daily tasks, as well as the significance of the potential impact of improving the effectiveness of their daily tasks, the organizational results that could be achieved over time are undeniable!

To make this more applicable, let us explore what this sort of translation would look like in healthcare. Most hospitals have a goal for minimizing harm, including decreasing their surgical site infection (SSI) rates in the operating room (OR). Many ORs leave the translation at something like, all staff in the OR have their personal goal to decrease SSIs. If they meet the goal, they don't have any real ownership in this win other than any financial bonus. If they don't meet this goal, they feel like they are being punished because they don't know what they did or didn't do to cause them to miss the goal. Either way, it is a meaningless goal that is actually counterproductive to the organization's culture and to staff engagement. The reason for the futility of this goal is due to the multifactorial nature of SSIs! There are literally hundreds of individual contributing factors that lead to an SSI. When an infection occurs, it is extremely difficult, if not impossible, to determine a root cause for this particular infection. There is a delay in time between the error or cause and when the infection manifests itself, and determining the root cause (or causes) is extremely difficult. At the same time, there are countless controlled studies and best practices that demonstrate why a particular approach or best practice is correlated to reduced risks of SSIs. Each of these represents a countable and relatively straightforward task or activity that can be tracked and measured (compared with a retrospective root cause analysis study on each SSI!). If we consistently do each of these specific evidence-based activities consistently, the literature and evidence support that these will have a quantifiable impact on the SSI rate in our OR.

Let's now take a look at a hypothetical organization that is the equivalent to the example from Cape Canaveral and President Kennedy's visit. A hospital CEO goes into the OR and asks a housekeeper what their job is, and they respond in the following way: "My job is to minimize surgical site infections, and I am on the front line of protecting patients and ensuring that they don't get infections!" Upon asking more questions, the CEO learns how they minimize SSIs and finds out that their manager collaborated with the quality and infection control departments to establish standard work and best practices for the housekeeping staff to use, which were integrated into their huddle boards. Also, their personal goals included metrics on adherence to their standard work and periodic surveillance and validation of their work, including aspects such as adherence to the product-specified dwell time of their antimicrobial solution, cleaning sequence, terminal clean process adherence, and other related (and countable) aspects of the process. Infection control had helped communicate the evidence-based best practices, which conveyed the *why* behind the *what* to the housekeeping staff. Periodic meetings of small teams of housekeeping managers and frontline staff and infection control helped to continuously improve the process and reinforce the significance of their work (the Hawthorne effect), as well as senior leader rounding and engagement in the process. Without this sort of support system and alignment, the SSI and overall harm goal would have been essentially a meaningless goal that didn't impact any substantial attainment of the strategy or goal, but instead it was manifested in a living, breathing, and active system that was taking very defensible and real steps toward improving patient care and outcomes and achieving the strategic goals of the organization! Even more importantly, this system helped empower the frontline staff who had never been engaged in this way, and provided them with context, meaning, and significance to their work, which they had never experienced before. The staff truly felt that their work mattered, as well as their ideas and thoughts. It is respect for people in action! It is at the heart of the TPS!

Catch-Ball Sessions to Help Negotiate Meaningful Goals: Where the Rubber Meets the Road!

Now that we have discussed the mechanics of goal alignment and aspects of goals that are critical (SMART goals), it is important to discuss when and where these goals are actually determined and negotiated. These are called "catch-ball" sessions and will be described in the following sections.

What Is a Catch-Ball Session?

Catch-ball might sound like a game, but it is actually a very simple (but critical) approach to addressing a common and very damaging dysfunction that occurs in almost all organizations when it comes to goal setting and evaluation. When goal setting is done in most organizations between a manager and direct reports, it is not a two-way discussion or a collaborative approach. It is often done *to* the direct report. It is not a meaningful two-way discussion resulting in the meaningful, translated, and aligned goals that Hoshin planning is seeking to get. This disconnect could prevent the ultimate goal of Hoshin planning from occurring before it even starts—so there must be a better way!

What Takes Place before a Catch-Ball Session?

Before a catch-ball session takes place, it is important that both the direct report and the manager or supervisor do some preparation to make the most of their time. If this isn't done, it is possible that much of the first catch-ball session will be wasted with discussions that could have been addressed prior to the session. If this preparation work wasn't done, then it is still a useful time to discuss and complete this preliminary work, but it is highly unlikely that the catch-ball session will result in finalized goals or meaningful agreement on a plan. By doing the prework beforehand, each of the two people at the catch-ball session have sat down and given some meaningful thought to the goal setting, their questions and concerns about the process, and a vision of what they want to accomplish during the next year.

To properly prepare for a catch-ball session, the following tasks should be completed by the listed people:

Manager or supervisor
- Complete, or substantially complete, the catch-ball session and form with their manager or supervisor. The catch-ball or Hoshin process is linear and iterative, where the goals established at a higher level are cascaded down through the organization. The result of the previous session becomes the "seed" of the next session. If it isn't completed, or the goals weren't done correctly, then the seed is unlikely to "sprout" and bear fruit! Sometimes managers or supervisors look at this process as a "check-the-box" activity and don't do it linearly and skip steps, which results in different catch-ball sessions with Hoshin goals that aren't aligned or linked, which defeats the whole point of Hoshin!
- Provide the most recent version of the Hoshin form to your direct report, so they have some idea of your goals going into the first session and have time to prepare and do some preliminary goal alignment. If the manager's or supervisor's goals aren't provided until the first session, then much of the session will be wasted with simply reviewing goals that could have been shared beforehand.
- Prepare a thoughtful explanation of the context and importance of your goals, how they are critical to the organization, and how your direct report is a critical piece in helping you achieve your goals, as well as helping the overall organization to be successful. This

succinct, thoughtful, and meaningful narrative is very motivational and an important piece of the Hoshin or catch-ball process. It helps provide further meaning to the *why* behind the *what* and move farther away from the check-the-box mentality that is so rampant in organizations as related to goal setting!

– Try to anticipate what questions, concerns, pushback, and areas of flexibility you have with your proposed cascading of goals. Some goals are nonnegotiable and need to be shared or distributed in a very specific way (such as when an organization is in crisis, or when there is no other way to distribute the responsibility), while other goals are negotiable. If you go into the session with no flexibility (room for negotiation), then it won't be a catch-ball session at all and this will defeat the entire point of the Hoshin process! If the staff member feels that this process is being done "to them" rather than in a collaborative way, then the critical buy-in, healthy relationship between a manager and their direct report, and meaningful improvement being driven throughout the year will be lost.

– Be prepared to explain how the Hoshin or catch-ball process is different than normal goal setting, why it is important, how the initial catch-ball sessions will work, how there will be ongoing meetings throughout the year (on a regular basis), and how this will benefit your direct report. Even though there will be organization-wide training and support for Hoshin planning, there will still be staff that "fall between the cracks" and don't get the training or education for one reason or another, or need further explanation and training just-in-time (JIT).

Direct report

– Before the catch-ball session, the direct report should have received their manager's complete (or substantially complete) Hoshin form with the goals of their manager or supervisor drafted. This will give the direct report an opportunity to familiarize themselves with their manager's goals. The catch-ball session isn't intended to have surprises or "gotcha" moments—it's meant to have meaningful two-way discussion, compromise, and mutual buy-in and understanding of the goals!

– Based on the goals of their manager or supervisor, formulate a preliminary draft of goals that are meaningful to the direct report and align to their manager's or supervisor's goals. These can be very rough, but at least form a foundation for discussion. Along with these goals, they should take notes on their rationale for why these were set the way they were, any questions or concerns they have, and anything else related to this that they would like to discuss during the session.

- Make a list of "other activities" to discuss with your manager or supervisor to hopefully free up some additional capacity (most staff are spread too thin and not focused coming into catch-ball sessions, so the catch-ball process actually starts to clear less strategic work off the staff members' plate) of the direct report away from meaningless, inappropriate, or nonaligned activities. By thinking through this and doing a "brain dump" onto paper beforehand, if there is pushback from the direct report that "there aren't enough hours in the day to do my job *and* all these goals," then these other activities become a fruitful discussion point on how to come up with a meaningful path forward. These other activities will be discussed in more detail in a later section.
- Make a list of any questions or concerns that the direct report has about the details of the Hoshin or catch-ball process, the ongoing regular meetings throughout the year to discuss progress toward the goals, and any particular personal or other discussion points.
- List any personal development goals, such as education, cross-training, promotion or leadership opportunities, technical certification, public speaking, or other similar goals. While these sorts of goals are personal and do not necessarily align, there may very well be situations where these personal development goals will align with organizational goals or priorities. Also, over time, as your "foundation" of the Toyota house is strengthened, there will be an increasing use of cross-training. As the cross-training is further developed in the organization, it adds a very discrete, tangible, and intuitive personal development goal for employees, as well as naturally integrating with succession planning, which is critical to long-term organizational success.

Now that we have discussed the necessary preparation for a Hoshin catch-ball session, we will now discuss in detail what a catch-ball session is, how it is different than normal goal-setting discussions, and how to make it successful.

A catch-ball is a physical item (such as a ball or something similar) that is passed between a manager and a direct report as essentially a "talking stick." It is an inanimate object that is used as a coaching tool to help teach, and foster a more productive and positive relationship (specifically during the Hoshin goal-setting process). If a manager and a direct report have a healthy, trust-based relationship, then during goal setting and the negotiation session, the direct report will feel open to "pushing back" against their boss's goal, and the boss will feel comfortable negotiating and discussing their needs and shared goal that they are asking their direct report to help with. If they don't, it is essentially a one-way discussion, with the direct report being told what their goals are, and with any pushback being "shot down" by their manager. The direct report is having an internal narrative with their boss that is verbalized, for example, "That is completely impossible to achieve with everything else I have going on! It doesn't matter anyways. My boss won't ask about these goals until next year and I know that he likes me, so I will get a good evaluation. Also, there are no bonuses anyways, so my evaluation doesn't matter and there is no real promotion opportunity for me, so I really don't care!" With one of the core Lean wastes being not utilizing employee creativity and the tremendous intelligence, experience, education, and knowledge in a healthcare organization, having our staff being this disconnected from strategy and not believing in or working on their goals throughout the year is a tragic and costly waste. It is no wonder that most organizations are so ineffective at goal attainment and weak at achieving their strategic plan! In this "current state," you could make a strong argument that strategic planning without meaningful translation and deployment (Hoshin planning) is a significant organizational waste!

In a true catch-ball session, the catch-ball is passed back and forth, and whoever is holding the catch-ball is the only one allowed to speak—without interruption! It helps to prevent the manager or direct report from interrupting the other participant in a potentially contentious and/or emotionally charged negotiation or discussion of goal setting. It helps to demonstrate a positive two-way discussion and negotiation rather than a one-way telling of goals. If the manager and direct report already have a trust-based relationship and there is true, open, meaningful discussion, then the catch-ball will just be a reminder of or reinforce the discipline of this. For the dysfunctional manager–direct report relationship, a catch-ball will be critical, but not by itself (remember, hope is not a plan)! Just like most "artifacts" such as this, if they are not coached and mentored by a mentor (or sensei), they will be just that—an inanimate object that is meaningless, or even destructive! With an experienced Hoshin coach or mentor facilitating the discussion, they can see when the proper back-and-forth negotiation is taking place, and the coach will help demonstrate and enforce the discipline of the catch-ball. At the beginning of the session, the coach or facilitator will describe the catch-ball process, the "rules of engagement," the use of the catch-ball, and the fact that there may have to be more than one catch-ball session. Also, the facilitator will ask about whether the initial goal-setting worksheet and thoughts have been done beforehand (see the Hoshin worksheet in Figure 2.1). Once this has been reviewed, the session is set to begin!

The manager or leader usually starts and describes the goals that they have negotiated with their manager or boss, the context of the organization, and the importance of their goals to the organization's viability, strategy, and future. Also, they will describe how these goals are shared among multiple direct reports, and that there is a "divide-and-conquer" approach that is critical to goal achievement.

With that completed, the catch-ball session is set to begin! After the manager or supervisor has conveyed the goals they have and their thoughts on the goals for their report, as well as conveying the contextual information, the catch-ball (a ball, or anything that is meaningful or helps to serve this simple purpose) passes to the direct report, and they now have an opportunity to provide their thoughts, goals, concerns, ideas, and other relevant aspects of the discussion. In a properly prepared for and executed session, both the manager and the direct report have done their homework. Also, enough information has been shared with the direct report (including the goals of the manager or supervisor that resulted from their catch-ball session with their manager) to allow them to go into the meeting ready to "push back," modify, challenge, or provide alternatives to.

Once they have had an opportunity to fully voice their thoughts and feedback, the catch-ball now goes back to the manager or supervisor, who should now have a better understanding of the level of buy-in and engagement of their staff in helping them achieve their goals. If it is a thoughtful and engaged leader, they will next work to help find "middle ground" to get closer to achieving true buy-in, engagement, and ownership of the goals with their direct report, while still working to make sure they are being challenged enough to help move the organization forward toward their strategic goals, as well as develop their direct report. This development is a critical aspect of a Lean system, as respect for people and developing leaders and staff in the organization is arguably at the very heart of Lean or TPS.

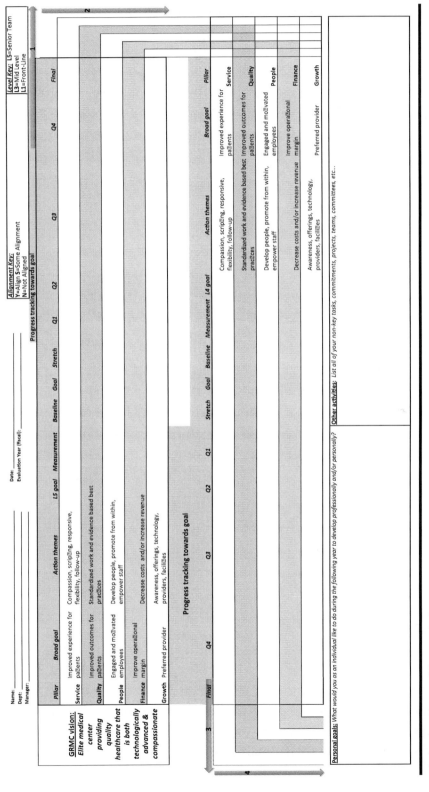

Figure 2.1   Hoshin worksheet.

Developing People with Hoshin (Respect for People Pillar of the Toyota House)

With this "people development" aspect in mind, building a Lean system should, over time, become increasingly integrated, holistic, and intertwined. For example, one of the strategic goals of the organization may (and should) be to develop increasing degrees of internal process improvement bandwidth and expertise, as well as developing and hardwiring the LDM system organizational and individual goals with process improvement, waste elimination, and other aspects of a holistic Lean system or TPS. If there was a goal of having a certain "penetration" of LDM boards, or developing a certain level of internal process improvement or Lean bandwidth and expertise in the organization, then this could be very readily translated through the Hoshin planning process and deployed within an organization. If a manager had 10 different direct reports, he might have negotiated a goal with his manager to have LDM boards in 6 of the 10 departments by the end of the year, and have these teams huddling a minimum of five times a week. He could then pace this out through the year and have a goal to "stand up" an LDM board in his department every two months through the year, resulting in six boards being "up and running" by the end of the year. This would be a SMART goal that would develop his staff and teams, reap organizational and improvement benefits for years to come, develop the manager by challenging them to get these LDM boards "stood up," and also integrate closely with the higher-level goals and with the manager's manager having a goal to round with a certain frequency and stay engaged with all these boards. The manager could also set a goal for LDM leader rounding, development of leader daily discipline documentation and standard work, and doing A3s, 5S projects, and other improvement work. This would be yet another aspect of aligning and supporting a holistic Lean system or TPS!

Other Activities (Clearing Our Staff's Plate to Drive Strategically Aligned Goals)

A "bottleneck" that can occur during the Hoshin process is that very meaningful goals are identified and negotiated between a manager and their direct report, but there are just not enough hours in the day or days in the week to get them done! While the core work they do may be causing this, often there is a much more actionable issue at play that can be brought to the surface and addressed through the Hoshin process.

In almost all organizations, there is an accumulation of random activities, committees, reports, commitments, projects, and other potentially "noncore" work that is often essentially "legacy activities" that have accumulated over the years and never went away. For example, if there was an initiative five years ago that resulted in a report requirement for your direct report, then the periodic generation of this report continued on indefinitely even though the project ended! Another example is you changed jobs four or five times within the same organization, and a small number of random tasks or commitments have followed from your old role to your new role. Over time, these accumulate to a potentially crippling (but not immediately obvious) level, because your core work may take up 80% of your time, and these random tasks take up the remaining 20%—and this remaining 20% of your time is what is absolutely critical for being able to focus on improvement work (such as working toward the organization's strategic goals). Therefore, this random noncritical or noncore work is getting in the way of allowing you and your direct reports from working on your goal attainment and Hoshin goals, or LDM boards, or Leader rounding—so the unintended cost of these is huge!

To help address this, it is critical for your direct reports (and for you) to document and review these other activities—basically a brainstorming of all the noncore things that and your direct reports are doing. After completing this, when you are having the Hoshin session with your direct report and there is some pushback along the lines of "That is a great goal and I would love to work on it, but there are not enough hours in the day!" you can review this list with them. There will surely be a number of items you can help your direct report stop doing, or reduce the scope or shift to a more appropriate person (carefully and tactfully) so that they are now able to have the bandwidth to work on their Hoshin goals. If you don't do this, there will be a paradox of asking your staff to do something that there isn't enough time to do, and there is no way around this. By documenting these other activities, you are able to "take something off their plate" and free up their time. This is empowering your direct report, shows respect to them, and helps them to understand that you are negotiating, compromising, and working to make this a win–win. Thinking about this in another way, this is also a great way to get buy-in to the Hoshin process. The staff no longer sees this as being a process that adds work through assignment of new or challenging goals, but rather as one that actually frees up their time and takes some things off their plate. Now that is a powerful tool for alignment and cultural transformation!

Chapter 3

Hoshin Goal Setting, Tracking, and Management

But How Do We Accomplish These Goals?

Now that we have established and translated meaningful goals and worked to achieve buy-in, the big question is, "How do we achieve these goals?" The best, most meaningful and translated goals are just "words on paper" or in a computer and meaningless unless there is motivation, oversight, account-ability, transparency, and meaningful ways to support progress and problem solving toward these goals! This is where the other aspects of Lean daily management (LDM), leader rounding, visual management, Lean projects, and the LDM boards come into play! They are a highly effective and flexible system for support and encouragement, and for leaders to stay involved and aware of their team's and team members' goal progress and efforts.

There are numerous aspects of Lean and LDM that are highly effective at supporting the aligned and meaningful goals that were created through the Hoshin planning process, and these will be explored in the following:

Monthly meetings with your manager or supervisor to reassess prog-ress toward goals, identify barriers and next steps, and keep focused on improvement. All of us (including myself) sometimes fall into a bad habit of procrastination, and only working on "what is in front of us" at the moment. With something like annual goals, it is easy to forget about or de-prioritize these until we are "under the gun" after almost all the year has gone by and our next review is upon us! At this point, it is really too late, as well established and truly SMART goals can't be accomplished overnight and require a lot of experimentation, hard work, and problem solving. By doing something as simple as setting up regular monthly meetings with your manager or supervisor, it keeps goals "on our radar" and helps maintain a "productive level of stress" to keep moving forward on the goals. At these regular meetings, barriers; progress (or lack thereof); changes in personal, organizational, or other priorities; and other relevant topics are discussed. This helps maintain a more regular focus on the goals, minimizes the amount of time between discussions, maintains a healthier ongoing relationship between staff members and their manager, and moves away from the "gotcha" cycle of not looking at goals more than once per year and then having very difficult and awkward discussions at the end of the year, where the manager may be in trouble for not achieving their goals, and then the direct report is under attack from the manager. Ironically, the manager had sent a strong signal to their direct report that this wasn't a priority because it hasn't been asked about since the last meeting.

If you are a manager or supervisor, you are probably thinking at this point, "Sure, that sounds great, but who has time to meet with each of their direct reports every month to go over goals? I have so much going on and so many crises that require fires to be put out that I can barely get through the day!" You are exactly right—right now you can't—because problems are rising to their highest level (you!) to be solved rather than being solved at the lowest level possible, with only select problems rising to your level to be solved. This is because you don't have an LDM system in place, which is highly effective at facilitating problems to be solved at their lowest level possible, thus freeing up managers and supervisors to focus their efforts on developing and supporting their staff, working on strategic and innovative initiatives, growing the business, and improving processes—which is what managers and supervisors (leaders) should be focusing on, rather than the "firefighting" that is currently getting in the way of doing these critical activities! As mentioned previously, one of the fundamental Lean wastes is not utilizing the creativity and experience of our staff (people), and developing an LDM system helps target this waste, but it also frees up our managers and supervisors to be true leaders rather than firefighters! Surprisingly, eliminating the waste of not utilizing our employees' creativity also results in eliminating much of the waste of not utilizing our leader's creativity and problem-solving ability and talents. Your leaders surely have this creativity and problem solving, which was one of the reasons that they were promoted and selected to be a leader in your organization.

Focus on back-of-the-envelope measurements that are not time-consuming but allow you to understand the effectiveness of changes. In order to achieve the Hoshin goals, it is critical (except with the project management and tasks previously discussed) to stay away from just guessing and making changes that may or may not be effective. We want to focus on the fundamental plan–do–check (or study)–act (PDCA) cycle, which is at its core a form of the scientific method. Without data or a feedback mechanism to test the effectiveness of our countermeasures (i.e., changes we are trying out), we are just guessing and there is a fundamental breakdown of our LDM system. We need to keep refocusing our teams on the "back of the envelope," or counting or frequency data that isn't perfect but allow us to gain enough insight or understanding of a process or issue that requires extremely time-intensive data gathering to get perfect data, or where there is no data available. Teams often default to thinking that we need perfect data (or large-sample-size data), which is probably driven by previous managers who challenged or questioned the validity of the less than perfect data they saw. This then drove teams to skipping data gathering altogether and just "acting" without validating. To avoid this trap, we as leaders need to encourage our teams to gather this back-of-the-envelope data as much as possible. During the LDM leader rounding, as well as during the periodic Hoshin planning meetings, it is critical that we always ask them for some form of at least rudimentary quantification of the effectiveness of what they are doing. If they aren't doing this (either teams or individuals), it is a perfect "early warning system" to identify a breakdown in the health of the LDM system and a great opportunity to step in as a leader and help to reinforce this critical gap in their thinking and problem solving. If there is no data being gathered or quantification of results, there is a breakdown in our LDM (i.e., scientific method) approach to problem-solving our way to achieving our strategic goals!

Goal Setting and Catch-Ball: Negotiating Goals for Improvement and Buy-In

Goals should follow the SMART goal framework (described previously) as closely as possible, and the catch-ball process strives to strike a balance between inherent biases and tensions that exist between a manager or supervisor and a direct report, which will be discussed in the next section. At the core of this is a significant component of the WIIFM principle: "What's in it for me?"

Managers naturally want to set aggressive "stretch" goals to drive the greatest improvement, but sometimes these are too aggressive and the team feels that they are unachievable, which is de-motivating. The manager or supervisor thinks that by mandating it, it will somehow happen on its own, and doesn't realize that this makes the entire goal-setting process meaningless if the direct report doesn't see that it is achievable or meaningful. It doesn't motivate improvement and simply creates stress and a tension and divide with their manager. The WIIFM for the manager is that they want to achieve and meet their goals, which will make them look like strong and effective leaders in the organization. This explains why they often set overly aggressive (and likely unachievable) goals for their staff. Therefore, the WIIFM is actually being sabotaged by their own overzealousness! If they truly want to achieve and look like strong leaders for their organization, they need to learn a new way of leading, goal setting, and management, which is LDM integrated with Hoshin or catch-ball!

Just like their managers or supervisors, direct reports rely heavily (just like any rational person would) on the WIIFM principle, but from a different perspective. When a manager or supervisor sets an overly aggressive (and likely unachievable) goal that the direct report doesn't believe in, they see this (rightfully so) as setting them up to fail. Therefore, they really have little or no incentive to work hard on achieving this goal. If they put in the extra effort to do this, they will still likely fail. Based on past organizational experience, they probably believe (rightfully so) that the organization and their manager's or supervisor's goals and priorities will shift or they won't think this is a priority much longer. Therefore, it is in the direct report's best interest to basically ignore the goal. This doesn't help the manager or supervisor, or the organization as a whole, so this lack of engagement and buy-in of the direct report short-circuits the whole goal-setting process, and ensures that the WIIFM for the manager or supervisor and the organization is not realized. Therefore, it is in the best interest of the entire organization to embrace the Hoshin or catch-ball process, and that there is significant achievement of the WIIFM for all involved.

With regards to employee-established goals, which are at the opposite extreme of managers setting unrealistic or unachievable goals, there is another dysfunction that relates to the WIIFM principle. Some managers or supervisors probably realized a while ago that the goal-setting process is substantially meaningless in their organization, and simply have employees set their own goals (which only get a cursory review from their manager or supervisor). When this occurs, the WIIFM for the direct report is to "set themselves up for success" in terms of the bureaucracy of their healthcare organization's human resources system, but not move the overall organization toward its goals or meaningful improvement. That is, they want to set goals that are very achievable, but usually (unless the staff member is highly self-motivated and/or competitive) lead to just "tasks" or goals that don't drive improvement. They basically set the bar very low and have goals that they know they will achieve (or already achieved!). At the end of the year, they will meet their goals, get their raise, or get a promotion. With the goals being self-set by the direct report, this is very rational for the direct report—honestly, many of us would do the same if we were given the chance, because we all want to succeed and get an A! Unfortunately, if everybody in an organization sets goals this way and everybody gets an A, then the organization as a whole is surely not going to get an A for its achievement of annual or strategic goals!

Finding Middle Ground

Therefore, we can see that neither manager- or supervisor-established goals (management by objective [MBO]) nor direct-report self-established goals are going to lead to meaningful alignment, achievement, and improvement—the WIIFM principle for each of these two parties sabotages the process and ensures that nobody wins in the long run.

The Hoshin or catch-ball process is a highly effective way of finding this middle ground, and over time, all members of the organization start to see more WIIFM in the new process! The catch-ball process is a way for negotiating the critical middle ground between staff and leadership for goals that drive improvement, but are achievable and the staff believes in. It is striking that a natural balance of "productive stress" is critical, as too little stress leads to apathy and "going through the motions," while too much stress is crippling. Organizations that commit to learning and implementing this new Hoshin process, integrated with an active LDM system, begin to see that the only way to achieve and be on the offense (as opposed to being on the defense and reacting to crises) as an organization is to utilize the creativity and problem solving of their leaders and staff, and establish and stay focused on long-term goals that don't waver. If the goals aren't set effectively, with a productive level of stress established for the direct report, coupled with buy-in from both parties, and ongoing, flexible, and supportive engagement by the manager or supervisor, then they are an exercise in futility.

Catch-Ball Goal Setting Creates a Pull for Data-Driven Goals from Staff

Another critical note on effective goal setting is that being successful at this requires investigation, "number crunching," and a meaningful two-way discussion with your manager. Just like with LDM boards, there is often a "vacuum" of meaningful data related to critical organizational problems and improvement opportunities, and this affects goal setting as well. It is critical that we set data-driven goals as much as possible (remember the SMART criteria we discussed earlier—if you don't, review quickly, as it is critical to this discussion), and the catch-ball back-and-forth with the manager or supervisor and the direct report needs to include discussion of how to effectively (and efficiently) measure the improvement goals we are setting. If we don't focus on this, then we are likely to get to the end of the year and say, "The process feels better," but we can't quantify it. This isn't a good way to run a healthcare organization or to develop our people, and it rarely leads to goal achievement. We need to encourage the back-of-the-envelope data collection that we discussed earlier, as this will pay off handsomely in terms of effective goal setting and achievement of goals. Also, during the periodic update meetings that we will have throughout the year, we can discuss these metrics when asking, "How are we doing on goal X?" It also sets these goals up for being a great fit for the LDM boards, as well as for the scientific method or PDCA-style experimentation that is critical to improve all but the most trivial of process issues.

Chapter 4

Integrating Hoshin with Operations

It is critical to integrate Hoshin goals with improvement efforts on Lean daily management (LDM) boards and in 90-day action plans, and work on achieving goals as a group or team continuously over the entire year. In addition to the monthly meetings we just discussed, we want to focus as much of the problem solving as possible into small groups and problem-solving teams. There is rarely a problem that a single person can identify, problem-solve, and fix on his or her own. Also, during the Hoshin goal-setting process, many of the goals are shared between multiple staff (not unique to each staff member), so these are a natural fit as an improvement topic for their LDM board, so that all the members of a team that share a similar (or dependent) job continuously meet as a team and meet with their supervisor or manager throughout the year to work toward achieving their goals. Sounds great, doesn't it? Rather than a year of just "doing the work" and "fighting fires," the year is spent working together collaboratively as teams and with managers, and being on the offense, improving and growing the business!

With problems being solved at lower levels, an active and dynamic escalation system in place from the LDM boards, and staff working on their goals throughout the year, our managers and leaders will have much of their time freed up and will have time to meet with their staff on a monthly basis to review goals, round on LDM boards, develop their best staff as their "lieutenants" or successors, and grow and develop the business. Remember, at its core it is a fundamental shift from playing defense to offense through

1. Problem solving rather than firefighting
2. Moving problem solving to its lowest level
3. Freeing up our supervisors or managers to be true leaders (vs. an extra set of hands)
4. Focusing on improving and growing the business rather than just treading water

Also, the monthly Hoshin meetings between managers and staff don't have to be all one-on-one meetings. If staff that report up to a manager all share a lot in terms of annual goals, the regular meetings with the staff on their Hoshin goal progress could (and should) over time be closely aligned to their LDM board, so hardwiring the LDM leader rounding to regularly attend their staff's huddles would serve the same purpose as this—updates, feedback, escalation items, adjustment of goals, and the leader's attendance showing the staff that this is critically important to the manager or supervisor (because they are there and asking!). The one-on-one meetings with staff could be more focused on individual goals (such as personal development, education, and cross-training) and occur less frequently (such as quarterly instead of monthly). This would reinforce the concepts of integration and how critical LDM leadership rounding is to the development of an LDM system!

While most of this discussion has been on the problem-solving focus of LDM and Hoshin, there is often an equally important and challenging aspect of work (and goal achievement) that is often a significant gap in organizations that doesn't deal with problem solving directly, but can relate to annual goals and Hoshin. There is often a significant amount of task work for new projects and initiatives that must be completed in a specific sequence or by a certain date to prepare for an inspection or certification, to establish a new line of business, or another related activity. Many (or most) of these tasks don't require problem solving per se, but they do require ongoing focus and attention to help fight the procrastination tendency that basically all individuals and organizations suffer from to some extent. Remember the prioritization board that we discussed earlier. This prioritization board is a great mechanism for helping to keep teams focused on these tasks throughout the year to help them achieve their Hoshin goals and improve their organization through completion of these tasks that have been identified as being important to the organization's goals and objectives. If a department is having daily huddles, one of these huddles could be focused on these tasks and the prioritization board. In these prioritization LDM sessions, the primary problem solving would be on the sequencing, timing, and relative prioritization of these tasks, as well as team assignments, deadlines, and escalating items up the chain of command for help where it is needed. The continued focus and regular discipline of focusing on these tasks will be a tremendous help and facilitator to ensure continued progress and completion of these tasks. Also, the LDM leader rounds will reinforce the importance of these tasks to the organization and act as a further motivator, as well as being a regular and natural opportunity for escalation items to be presented and discussed with their leader. The performance metric for these sorts of projects would be schedule adherence and task completion rate, which could both be problem-solved if the project or rate of completion fell behind schedule. This turns this sort of project to an initiative that is amenable to LDM and problem solving and alignment to organizational strategy and goals, rather than just a collection of tasks!

Given the criticality of data to problem solving and goal achievement, reinforcing and encouraging teams to become experts and use their creativity and problem solving to develop innovative and novel ways is critical to success.

It is then critical to form small, multidisciplinary teams to help tackle problems in a collaborative way. As teams continue to practice their LDM sessions at their boards, a variety of different problems will "bubble to the surface" that can't be addressed "within the four walls of their department." Some of these will be escalation items that need to go to their manager, some will require large, multidisciplinary teams (that need strong leadership and facilitation), while others are small to medium-sized problems that require a multidisciplinary approach and involve outside departments. In most healthcare organizations, these small to medium-sized problems don't normally result in collaborative team problem solving. At best, they may result in standing meetings that don't accomplish anything. With the clearly defined Hoshin goals now in place, and teams becoming practiced in team-based A3 problem-solving approaches (using the simplified A3 structure inherent in the LDM board structure), the structure is now in place for ongoing and aligned improvement.

Step-by-Step Approach to Deploying Hoshin Planning and Linking It to Your LDM System

1. *Conduct top-level strategic goal setting as early as possible.* Invest as much time as you can as early as possible and receive as much feedback as you can! Most organizations wait too late to do this, and then take too long, and this doesn't give 95% of the organization enough time to work on their goals. If you don't do a good job at the top, it is "garbage in, garbage out" throughout the organization, as everybody is using these top-level goals in one way or another to translate, link, and cascade throughout the organization. If you do a great job at the top level and take too long, then most of the catch-ball sessions will just be "check-the-box" activities and will be largely wasteful for the organization.

2. *Develop a disciplined schedule for deploying Hoshin planning throughout your organization, allowing sufficient time for each level to have multiple catch-ball sessions.* Allow some slack time at the end just in case the process takes longer than expected, which it likely will early on!

3. *Train all leaders and managers in the organization in the Hoshin or catch-ball process so that they deeply understand it and how it is different from normal goal setting.* Demonstrate (with role playing) good and bad catch-ball sessions, and good and bad examples of filling out the Hoshin alignment form, periodic (quarterly) goal review sessions, and so forth.

4. *Work with human resources to integrate and streamline the "mechanics" of Hoshin with their existing goal-setting and performance evaluation systems* (or work to get appropriate software or systems to support Hoshin), and develop training and support resources for deploying in the organization. If there is an electronic annual goal-setting and performance management system (which most hospitals above a certain size will have), evaluate its ability to align and translate top-level goals all the way through an organization, update goals and show progress (or lack thereof) during the year, be flexible to adapt to unique departmental goals and challenges, and view the progress and effectiveness of Hoshin and catch-ball sessions, as well as goal attainment and regular meetings. If the current system is not supportive of this, don't delay starting the Hoshin process! Develop a manual Hoshin system of paper

forms (using the x-matrix as a guide; see Chapter 5) or another similar system to facilitate the process, and then deploy it in key areas for the first year or two. As soon as this system gap is identified, begin working on identifying a suitable vendor who has a product that will support your Hoshin efforts, and schedule demonstrations and ask them targeted questions related to the Hoshin process you are working to develop. Once you identify a vendor, budget this (it will be more than worth it!) and continue developing your system until the new one is in place to support it. If you find that your paper system (the work-around) is effective and drives meaningful goal setting and alignment and doesn't result in too much additional labor and resources, don't feel compelled to get a fancy electronic system! Just use the system that is already working! Toyota always recommends trying the "simple, little, no-cost" solution first and only going to more sophisticated solutions when the simpler solutions have been ruled out. Do the same in this case!

5. *In addition to any electronic goal-setting programs, it is critical to develop a Hoshin catch-ball form* (paper and pencil—just like doing an A3) that fits with your organization's terminology, pillar goals, and other unique characteristics (see Figure 2.1). These forms are extremely helpful for facilitating and capturing the real-time catch-ball discussions that take place. Some people may say that this isn't necessary and is a wasteful "extra step" because we already have a computer program to capture these. The reality is that, especially at first, there is as much struggle and difficulty with the goal-setting software as there is with the catch-ball form. The last thing we want is for the technology to distract and detract from the meaningful catch-ball discussion, as having the goals and alignment documented on a paper sheet allows for the struggle to make the goal information in a form to fit and be adapted into the software program. Also, it is very rare that any goal-setting program actually fits the outcome of the catch-ball session perfectly, so keeping the results of the form on record and updating periodically during the quarterly or more frequent update sessions throughout the year is a highly effective way to further facilitate these discussions. Just like most things with Lean or Toyota Production System (TPS), we want to always use the lowest-tech, lowest-cost solution first and only use technology when we are required to do so, or when it genuinely solves a problem that couldn't be solved any other way. Hoshin planning and using

pencil, eraser, and paper for the catch-ball sessions is a perfect example of this principle!

6. *Develop multiple Hoshin super users who have deep knowledge and experience with the Hoshin, goal-setting, and catch-ball process.* These "super users" will serve two primary uses:

   a. Facilitate the critical top-level strategic goal setting, as well as the C-suite or senior executive catch-ball sessions. These activities are few in number and absolutely critical to the success of the overall initiative due to the nature of org-charts being so narrow at the top and spreading out so widely at the bottom. As the goals cascade from few to many, errors or poorly composed or defined goals are amplified as they spread during the Hoshin process.

   b. These super users would also serve a critical role as internal coaches, mentors, and trainers for the embedded Hoshin coaches. Their much greater level of knowledge and experience would be critical for the embedded coaches to "borrow their learning curve," which is a common and critical theme of developing a Lean system—mentorship and guidance are critical! In addition to the mechanics of training, coaching, and mentoring the embedded coaches, these super users would also be benefitting from this second role as well: there is no better way to learn something yourself than to train, develop, and support others! Also, these super users went through the top-level goal setting, so they have critical knowledge and awareness of the top-level organizational goals (and associated context—the *why* behind the *what*), which can be conveyed and used to help support the embedded coaches in their work. These staff may very well (and probably will) be some of our Lean or TPS embedded coaches who are cross-trained as the Hoshin super users—the overlap in personalities, temperaments, and systems thinking with good Lean or TPS embedded coaches would be significant (and should be). This also helps support the spread and development of LDM boards, given the long-term alignment of LDM boards with Hoshin goals.

7. *Identify and train (through shadowing the Hoshin or catch-ball super users and other forms of instruction and guidance) embedded Hoshin coaches to attend or facilitate Hoshin sessions, provide feedback on the sessions, develop leaders and staff in becoming better goal setters and goal translators, and be overall organizational resources to support and integrate Hoshin.* Don't underestimate the importance of this! Just like

most things, Hoshin takes practice and is a big change for the organization and individuals within the organization. If it is not mentored and coached, it will just be "wallpaper" in that the forms and systems will just be corrupted to match the old way of goal setting, but with more steps and false pretenses (in this case, it would be better to have not done Hoshin than to do it half-heartedly). These embedded coaches would be located in different divisions, groups, departments, or areas, and would need dedicated time to be developed, and during the major "push" of goal setting would need to have their core positions "back-filled" to allow them sufficient time for this critical role. Even though this might temporarily cause a slight decrease in productivity, it will pay off handsomely for the organization that makes this investment! Another way to simplify this process, instead of having "no good deed go unpunished" by having departments and areas have (what appears to be) decreased productivity due to the dedicated Hoshin staff, is to have a separate department or charge code set up in the payroll system so that these staff can charge their hours to this different charge code (rather than ambiguously falling into decreased global productivity of the department). This has a second benefit as well: it allows for clear financial quantification of the financial investment in the goal-setting process. This is also a very good approach for charging hours of general Lean or TPS embedded coaches, where the issues are the same as having partially dedicated Hoshin coaches: the departments that identify to develop these staff and invest their time are "punished" in the accounting system for doing this, and this acts as a strong disincentive to the departments identifying and investing in their staff. When this counterproductive incentive system is fighting our efforts to develop our best people, our staff who are supposedly 25% "dedicated" to Hoshin or continuous improvement are constantly pulled into the day-to-day crisis management of the department and, in actuality, end up spending probably only 3%, or at most 10%, of their time working on Hoshin or Lean or TPS efforts, which is not sufficient to give them the requisite experience, knowledge, cycles of learning, or bandwidth to meaningfully benefit the organization to the extent intended. With a separate charge code, the amount of their work in these critical dedicated roles is much easier to quantify, and they are likely to be more accountable and able to "push back" against the pull for daily firefighting needs (due to the message the organization sent by formalizing the funding or support for these roles), and hold the staff more accountable for the outputs or results for their dedicated efforts. These embedded coaches will need to help train and facilitate dozens (or hundreds) of these sessions to become true "masters" of the catch-ball and goal-setting process, but once they are, their value to the organization on an annual and ongoing basis will be tremendous! Don't forget, this isn't just a "once-a-year" activity—there are quarterly (or more) review sessions that are a "refresher" on their goals, what has changed in the organization, and their progress (or lack thereof) toward these goals. Therefore, goal setting changes from being a once-a-year activity to being a continuous, ongoing effort (just like LDM boards) to encourage, align, and support progress toward the organization's strategic goals at all levels of the organizations—from the C-suite or board of directors all the way down to the front lines.

8. *Now that you have facilitated high-quality top-level goals, trained Hoshin or catch-ball super users, worked to set up your Hoshin forms and associated goal-setting software, completed awareness training for your staff and leaders, and established a timeline, you are in a great place to start a more broad rollout of Hoshin!* If your organization is of a size that is appropriate to be supported by the Hoshin super users, embedded coaches, and other resources identified and developed for rolling out Hoshin, then you can begin cascading your goals (through facilitated catch-ball sessions; remember, if you just assume that the meetings will go well, you are setting your organization up for failure during the upcoming year and helping to establish new bad habits!). If, like most organizations, you don't have enough dedicated resources to roll out Hoshin organization-wide (which is most organizations, because they underestimate the time that it will take to do these catch-ball sessions, especially given the fact that multiple sessions are usually required when first starting Hoshin), there is fortunately a great alternative that is recommended for most organizations—and that is in line with the Lean concept of establishing a "model line." Instead of organization-wide rollout, pick a few parts of the organization with strong and committed top-level support, and a strong "chain of command" all the way to the front lines. Make sure you *don't* pick your greatest challenge or an area where there are already deep-seated leadership or management issues! This is an *extremely* common mistake that organizations make, with Hoshin and process improvement in general. When an organization is just starting its journey (overall, or with a specific approach), you want to "set yourself up for success" to allow for organizational

and individual learning through the exercise, and to have a "go-and-see" area to demonstrate to the rest of the organization that "this works here—not just external examples that the consultant had or that I read about in the book." This is a very powerful change tool! You then take all the Hoshin or catch-ball resources that you developed for the organization (but weren't sufficient for organization-wide rollout) and concentrate them in this one area. Now you have enough resources to effectively support this more focused deployment! Remember, it is all about quality rather than quantity; we want to have successes and learnings coming from these activities—not just checking the box! The senior coach (sensei) will watch and help guide the super users and other coaches, and attend many of these sessions to help facilitate the sessions, as well as to continue mentoring and coaching the super users and embedded coaches. Once the sensei is confident (through real-life Hoshin observations) that the super users and embedded coaches are sufficiently trained and experienced "in the field," then they can let them learn and experience on their own now that they have a foundational knowledge.

9. *After completing this pilot phase of Hoshin or catch-ball through creating a model line and completing the goal setting, conduct a postdeployment Hansei session to reflect on what worked, what didn't work, and how you could do better next year.* This sort of reflection is absolutely critical! It allows us to continuously improve and adapt, which is critical to any organizational deployment or improvement effort. This would allow us to identify changes to forms and changes to our human resources goal-setting system, potentially change to a different software product, identify bandwidth issues with how many coaches we have, and establish better timelines for deployment, as well as a litany of other improvements and insights that we can use before we do hospital (or system-wide) deployment. During the next year, these same coaches and support resources will need to be closely monitored and supported to ensure that they continue to have the periodic sessions to review progress, identify successes, and identify barriers. As often as possible, you want these sessions to be facilitated by the same coaches who did the initial catch-ball discussions, because they possess the original context and knowledge of the goals. At the end of the year, doing Hansei (reflection) sessions with staff involved in Hoshin at all levels within this model line will provide an opportunity to help communicate the power and effectiveness of this approach to others in the organization.

"Verbatims" or testimonials help communicate (in a peer-to-peer fashion) what the experience was like, that it wasn't something to fear, that it led to increased job satisfaction and organizational "context" and meaning throughout the year, and that it resulted in kudos, successes, and positive accolades for the department that "stepped up to the plate" to be open to change, try a different approach, and take a risk. This approach of positive reinforcement is critical! Early adopters step up to the plate despite the uncertainty, and there are always departments and leaders who are more "wait and see" and skeptical based on personality, temperament, or negative previous experiences. When they hear that this approach is leading to positive outcomes and accolades to the leaders and staff, and that the organization's leadership is staying committed to this (and it's not just a "flavor of the month"), they are much more likely to be willing to accept and try it.

10. *Now that we have had a successful pilot of the Hoshin process, we take what we have learned in terms of mechanics and logistics, timing, coaching and support bandwidth, change management, accountability, and ongoing sessions throughout the year, and wrap these all together into a plan to deploy Hoshin more thoroughly throughout the organization.* With enough commitment and resources, you could deploy hospital-wide (or system-wide), but you will likely see during the model line pilot that it is more resource-intensive at first than originally thought. For example, each of the Hoshin or catch-ball sessions takes several sessions to do correctly, and certain areas will be much more difficult to do than others (due to the nature of the work, availability of metrics, or difficulties with multiple shifts or highly resistant leaders or staff). Setting the top-level goals correctly is often started too late and compresses the time for a huge number of staff to complete their sessions. If this is the case (as it is with most organizations—whether they believe it or not), continue to incrementally roll out the Hoshin to more and more parts of the organization, continuously refining the process, developing your bandwidth to support these efforts, and having a greater and more diverse set of internal examples and "wins" to help build a case for change for others in the organization (who are inherently more resistant than the early adopters). By taking this incremental approach, you are getting more wins earlier than you would have with an "all-in" approach, refining your process and bandwidth to properly support the efforts, and constantly reflecting to do better with each successive "wave" of Hoshin or catch-ball. This is also a highly effective

approach given the natural bell curve of people and departments. The early adopters are open to change and embrace the new process. The "middle of the curve" is more neutral and takes a wait-and-see attitude, which is supported by the success of the model or pilot line. By the time you get to the "other end of the curve," opposite the early adopters, you have greatly matured the process, support, mechanics, and case studies to make it much more difficult for these staff (who are almost pathologically resistant to change) to not at least try it, especially given that the organization and leadership are now fully engaged and supportive of this approach and it is clear that to not embrace it at this point would reflect very badly on their department and annual performance.

11. *Throughout this process of experimenting with Hoshin, deploying it in a pilot or model line, and then broading deployment, you want to be continuously integrating with competing initiatives, LDM boards, leader rounding, quality, and other process improvement initiatives.* As with any initiative, they are unlikely to survive alone "in a desert" and be seen as "just one more thing." If they are integrated with other initiatives and seen as being integral to an organization's strategy, survival, and health, then it is much easier to get appropriate levels of buy-in, support, and engagement. Over time, the content on the LDM boards will align more closely with the Hoshin goals, which are tied to the performance, merit, or incentive system, so there is a strong reason for the teams to be doing LDM. For the same reason, there will be strong incentives for leaders to round on the LDM boards and have their own LDM sessions, as rounding on these boards will be indiscernible from "going to the Hoshin gemba" and literally being able to walk through their chain of command at any time throughout the year and seeing where there are strengths, weaknesses, success, failures, and opportunities for them (as leaders) to support and engage with their teams. Integrating Lean projects with the LDM boards, which are also initiatives that are aligned with the Hoshin goals, is a further three-way alignment that is extremely powerful. This "weaving" is all part of developing "your organization's way" and not having different initiatives as separate or stand-alone pieces. It is over time integrating all of them into a meaningful whole!

Chapter 5

The Baptist Journey

The Baptist Health System in San Antonio, Texas began its Lean journey in 2008 and has implemented a management system that consists of four fundamental components: (1) performance, (2) process, (3) people, and (4) plans (Figure 5.1). These elements are not independent of one another. While they may be deployed at various times and vary in their strength, they support each other, and together they strengthen the Lean management system and therefore the organization. Ultimately, these elements support the Baptist journey toward high reliability.

Performance

Whenever you begin Hoshin, you start with the end goal in mind. In 2008, when I joined Baptist, we did not have a plan detailing our Lean journey for the next several years and how we would implement these elements. At Baptist, our Lean management system developed organically, around an end goal sought by our CEO of having a structure of continuous improvement that engaged more individuals throughout the organization. Lean was also new to health care, so we were learning how to bring Lean into a different industry. When we embarked on our Lean journey, we started with the element of performance.

The performance quadrant (Figure 5.1) consists of Lean tools used to improve the performance of an organization. Some of these tools include kaizen rapid cycle improvement event (RIE) events, 5S, visual management, standard work, poke yoke, quick changeover, kanban, and numerous

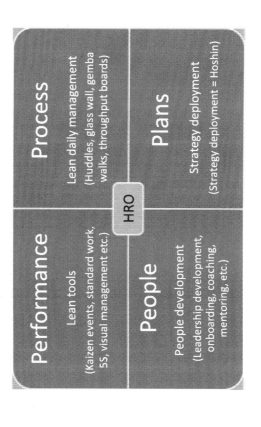

Figure 5.1 Baptist Health System Lean management system. High Reliability Organization (HRO).

other tools. They can be used by organizations along any spectrum of Lean maturity. Often, outside consultants may enter an organization and use these for targeted improvement efforts. These tools are very powerful and can result in improved performance metrics, but alone they do not develop a system of continuous improvement or develop people.

In the summer of 2009, we held a kaizen event that would capture the attention of both leaders and staff. While some were eager to learn and embrace Lean, others were skeptical of what this new approach could offer. A great way to earn support was to expose the power of a rapid cycle improvement event that would have enough impact to gain traction and endorsement for further development of the management system.

The emergency department was a great place to start! There was need for a patient flow redesign, as the system was experiencing high rates of patient walkout rates. Additionally, with such a high volume of daily visits, the emergency department was a great environment for the rapid testing of process changes. The kaizen event led to a system-wide redesign of four of the emergency departments, with up to 40% improvement in the length of stay, virtual elimination of emergency medical services diversion hours, and a 70% reduction in the walkout rate. Attention captured? Yes!

People

The second quadrant, people, is focused on people development. A highly functioning Lean organization (or high-reliability organization [HRO]) is *always* doing this. This can be exhibited through how you onboard new team members to how you coach direct reports, or during your leadership development retreats. People development should be sprinkled throughout your Lean journey, and you should never miss an opportunity to develop your people. Although our Lean journey did not start with large-scale leader training, we did not miss the opportunity throughout the emergency room kaizen to teach the team members. They learned about visual management and standard work without going to a class. They learned by being part of the improvement efforts!

By February 2009, Baptist was eager for more Lean exposure. The positive outcomes of the kaizen event were being felt throughout the organization and the leaders wanted more! The topic of the spring 2010 leadership conference was Lean and performance improvement. The session exposed several hundred leaders of the Baptist Health System to Lean fundamentals, including a simulation that used the lunch serving line as an experiment. Little did the leaders know that the misplaced serving utensils, the hap-hazard placement of food, and the maze of tables creating the horribly congested food line were a testing ground for their second kaizen event. I received a text during lunch from one of our vice presidents that read, "This line is a mess, you need to Lean this thing out!" After lunch, we exposed the leaders to the truth behind the flopped lunch; they were "had" and they loved it! The leaders began applying their newly learned Lean skills to rede-signing the lunch line and had the opportunity to experience their very own first Lean process redesign on day two of the conference.

I share the story of how Baptist started its Lean journey because it exposes two of my fundamentals that I stick by for just about any new proj-ect, change, strategic deployment, and so forth. My first fundamental strategy is understand the current environment and what would be the best fit. You need to be strategic in how you begin your Lean journey. When I started at Baptist, what was needed then to launch Lean was an attention-getting kaizen event followed by widespread sprinkling of Lean knowledge. Leaders needed to see it in action, learn it, experience it, and apply it!

My second fundamental strategy is have fun! We could have constructed a simulation of patient flow at the spring leadership conference, but we opted for something that *everyone* could relate to, eating lunch. Sure, they were frustrated, but when they saw the video, which was secretly recording from a corner of the room, they had a big laugh at the way they looked like mice in a maze. They never forgot this lesson, they had fun themselves, and to this day I still receive comments from people that were at the conference on how bad the lunch was and that they know "waste is bad."

Soon after the leadership conference at Baptist, we began training cohorts of Lean practitioners across the system on various tools. The opera-tional improvement department at Baptist consisted of two people, and we needed deeper bench strength. (In fact, the operational improvement department never had more than five employees over 10 years.) Our goal was never to grow a large market department supporting the health sys-tem, but rather to teach and coach and allow the leaders to teach and coach others. This not only helped us by having more coaches in the system, but also provided the leaders with knowledge to develop their teams, which helped to develop themselves. We needed a critical mass that would sup-port this. The Lean practitioners applied their new knowledge and com-pleted 5S projects across the system, implemented standard work, utilized visual management, mapped processes to better understand the issues, and targeted minimizing waste. We gave them eyes for waste. They learned that waste was "smoke to fire." If they saw waste, then something was not optimized and they would investigate. Sometimes the practitioners could tackle the problems, or if they were more complex, they would reach out to the engineers in the system operational improvement department. The goal of developing more people to have the tools isn't for all of them to be experts or lead large-scale projects on their own, but to continuously invest in our people and provide some basics that would benefit their department today, as well as provide a foundation for continued learning.

Process

The process quadrant contains the daily processes that become part of *how* the organization manages daily, the "kata." Kata are the rehearsed and practiced daily practices or habits that drive cultural change. For Baptist, this is everything under the daily management system, including huddles, gemba walks, glass wall, and throughput boards. These daily processes provide a structure to support operations and a framework for continuous improvement.

While the hospitals had conducted huddles for several years, they were inconsistent and lacked structure. In 2011, Baptist began daily facility huddles with a structure and agenda that supported transparency. It's important to note that there was structure to the new huddle, yet it still allowed for flexibility of the individual hospital and its needs. The purpose of the new huddle was not just to communicate the current state across all facility leaders, but also to share challenges and barriers, and safety concerns. The huddles improved communication across the organization and provided a mechanism to quickly report a safety concern so the team could ensure that it was addressed, learn from it, and make sure it was not repeated in the future. The huddles provided opportunities for "shout-outs," as well as a chance to ask for help on actions that need a quick turnaround. Another by-product of the huddles was that they introduced a daily cadence to the leaders that centered on communication, learning, and continuous improvement. These huddles integrated well into the developing management system.

With the huddles underway, as well as targeted training and performance improvement efforts, there was still a challenge: How do we develop *more* employees and engage all staff in continuous improvement? Additionally, it was difficult to sustain wins from the complex projects or improvement events taking place. The daily management system needed to extend into the departments of the hospital and where the work was done, the gemba, to alleviate these growing pains.

Lean daily management (LDM) gemba walks began at the first Baptist hospital in April 2013. The unit-level gemba boards provided the foundation to engage staff at the next level by providing a structure to rapidly test ideas, a place to share their learnings, and the infrastructure for daily continuous improvement. Back to the fundamentals previously mentioned, understand the current environment and what would be the best fit. Had we started our Lean journey with LDM, the level of buy-in would have been significantly less. The leaders supported Lean, they had seen what it could do for patient care and operations, and they trusted that this next progression in the journey would take them to the next level.

LDM requires a significant amount of leadership support to deploy and even more for continued sustainment. You can conduct kaizen events and training sessions with a moderate level of executive support; however, when you implement a daily management system, you need 100% support from your executives. The deployment is fun and leaders are eager to round on their units while learning the new tools. Like any change, the sustainment is the challenge. This was no different at Baptist.

I met with the CEO of the market and we discussed what it would take to implement and maintain. I had 110% of his support—it was the perfect time! As part of the deployment, we focused heavily on people development, development of the front line as well as the leaders. We could not expect our front line to participate in continuous improvement if they were not given the tools or provided the education and coaching. You can see that the elements of the Baptist management system do not exist in isolation and are more interwoven. The training for the frontline staff started as a two-day training in the first hospitals, and we were able to condense to one day based on feedback from staff and becoming more familiar ourselves with the training and launch. Additionally, as part of the implementation, all executive leaders attended a day of introductory training on LDM.

A lesson learned in the deployment of LDM was that we minimized the involvement of the directors. We were so focused on making the unit-level gemba boards frontline staff focused that we did not provide adequate training to the directors. This was a mistake. The directors need to lead their team and provide coaching to their team around their performance improvement journey. If anything, we realized that the directors needed more training and coaching than anyone else.

Over the next six months, all five facilities had implemented gemba boards and administrative teams were leading gemba walks. The first several months, departments tackled simple operational challenges and staff and leaders became familiar with how to use the tools. There were many quick wins throughout the facilities attributed to the use of gemba boards. The boards evolved over time, as we learned more about them and what worked best within our culture. Initially, boards were templated to contain five metrics, with one metric to align with each pillar of quality, service, operations, growth, and cost. *Lesson learned: Don't force a department to have a certain number of improvement metrics or monitoring metrics!* It should depend on the challenges facing the department at the time. If a unit is doing very well financially but is missing some of its quality metrics, wouldn't you want it to focus more on its quality? The quality of the metrics, the performance improvement activity, and the involvement of staff are more important than the quantity of metrics.

Over time, the boards evolved from just problem solving to containing both a monitoring and a problem-solving section (Figure 5.2). If a department was struggling in a couple of the pillars and excelling at another, then we often moved the achieved metrics to "monitoring only" if the unit wanted to continue to monitor performance. *Another lesson learned: It was important to have standard work and core elements at the gemba board to support problem solving, and this made it possible for the leaders to interact with boards across the system.* However, in the spirit of continuous improvement, the board structures themselves should and need to continuously improve. Another change to the board was adding the facility huddle notes. The board was a perfect place to communicate what took place at the daily facility huddle with the front line during their huddle. A gemba board needs to support the staff and fit into the needs and culture of the organization. The staff at Baptist helped to create phase II and eventually phase III gemba boards (Figure 5.3), and they embraced them more as they were part of their evolution.

As the departments matured in their use of the gemba boards, they began to tackle more complex issues that required interdepartmental collaboration. This was a challenge for the units, and we could see that the metrics selected were not complementary to those of other departments or to those of the hospital. The increased complexity of the problems required more coaching by the executives and directors. It is natural for leaders to want to solve problems for their staff, and while this is great in certain situations, it does not fully engage the staff in continuous improvement. A technique our

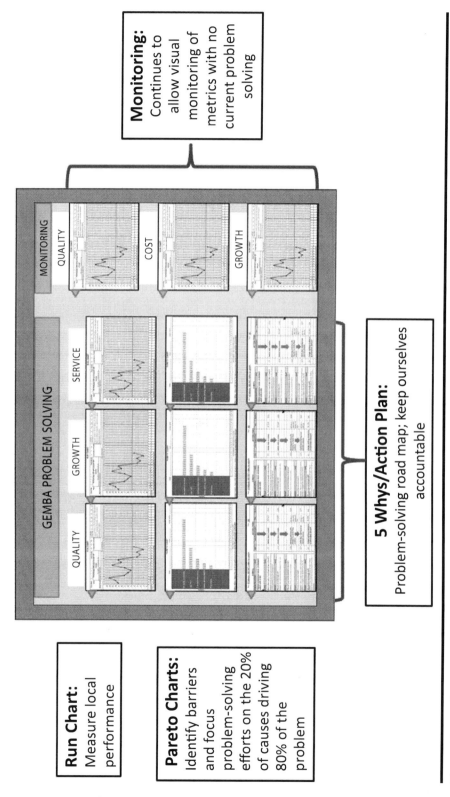

Figure 5.2 Phase II unit-level gemba board structure with monitoring section.

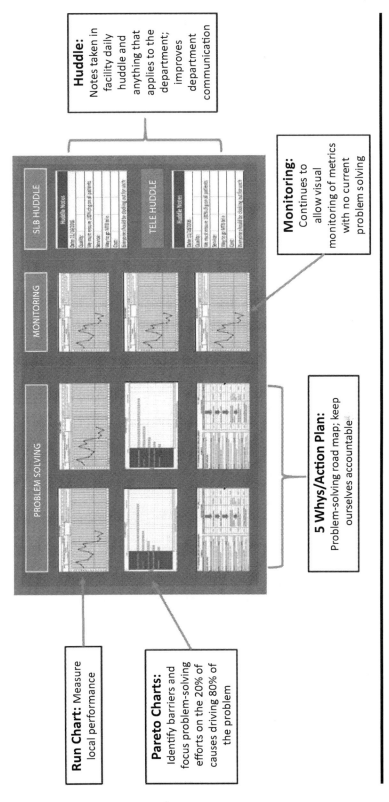

Huddle: Notes taken in facility daily huddle and anything that applies to the department; improves department communication

Monitoring: Continues to allow visual monitoring of metrics with no current problem solving

5 Whys/Action Plan: Problem-solving road map; keep ourselves accountable

Run Chart: Measure local performance

Pareto Charts: Identify barriers and focus problem-solving efforts on the 20% of causes driving 80% of the problem

Figure 5.3 Phase III unit-level gemba board with huddle notes.

leaders had to embrace was *how* to coach their teams through solving the problem; therefore, we spent the next few months focused on developing our leaders' coaching skills. This entailed group sessions, one-on-one sessions, and shadowing of the leaders during gemba walks to provide support. Baptist developed a coaching kata and included open-ended questions for the leaders to use. Open-ended questions are always encouraged in coaching to prompt staff in discussion rather than giving an option of simply stating yes or no. Questions the leaders should ask are: *What is the goal you are trying to achieve? How are we doing? What obstacles are you facing? What are your next steps?* Over time, staff anticipates the types of questions asked, and they will provide the information outright. At this stage, the interaction between the leaders and staff becomes more comfortable and the leaders have an opportunity to learn more about the department, the problems they are tackling, and the staff.

With the leaders armed with this new skill set, they were better prepared to support their departments. However, the departments were still not aligned in their targeted performance improvement indicators. In response to this situation, Baptist began deployment of glass wall to provide a framework that would align goals throughout the facility and move the organization in a common direction. Glass wall is part of the daily management system and is a literal wall of metrics that displays the hospital's most important goals to be worked on at that time (Figure 5.4). Glass wall later evolved to become part of the overall Hoshin process. Glass wall in its infancy was targeted at what needed improvement right now, not long-term plans or targeted improvement deadlines. It began to show the directors throughout the hospital the priority areas visually and frequently, and subsequently the directors worked with their departments on how they could impact these metrics.

At Baptist, the glass wall contained lagging indicators selected by the executive team based on the system goals and the facility's current performance to these goals. These lagging metrics were attached to department-level leading metrics. For example, a glass wall metric may be to reduce catheter-associated urinary tract infection (CAUTI) rates or central line–associated bloodstream infections (CLABSIs) by a certain percentage. The department will have a leading metric on its unit-level gemba board that supports achievement of the lagging metric on the glass wall, such as compliance with catheter bundle components.

In the first year, we went through several iterations of glass wall and how best to use and interact with it. Should it be reviewed daily with all directors

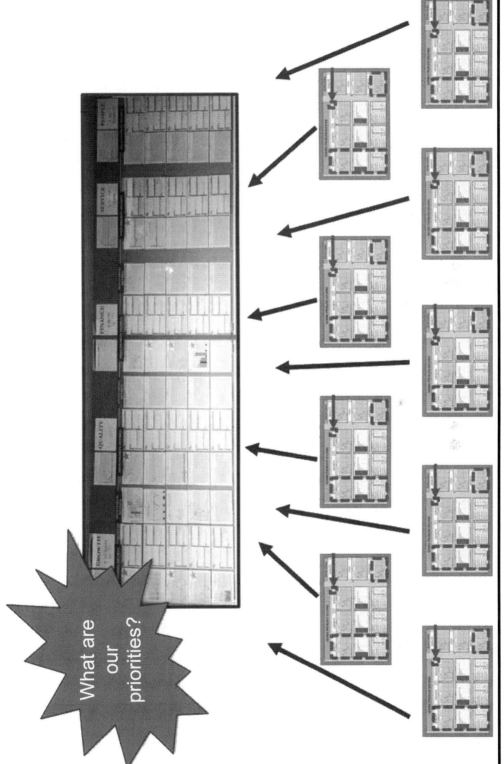

Figure 5.4   Glass wall: main business indicators organized by pillar and LDM gemba board alignment.

and the administrative team, or weekly among just the executive team? The answer is, "It depends." Just like the gemba boards, we worked with each of the facility leadership teams and integrated glass wall into their leadership style and culture. Some facilities chose one pillar for each day of the week for review at their facility huddle. Others only reviewed targeted metrics that had actions due.

Certain facilities and departments modified the LDM gemba walk now that they had a glass wall and created "group boards." Executives would huddle with their direct reports at the group boards and review progress on metrics that align with the glass wall, while the director would then huddle with their frontline staff at their department-level gemba board (Figure 5.5).

Glass wall provided a mechanism for Baptist to align goals within the hospitals and across the system. Many clinical initiatives became system-level targets, and through glass wall as part of the management system, Baptist was able to achieve significant improvements. It experienced reductions of up to 60% in CAUTIs, *Clostridium difficile* infections, and CLABSIs. Some facilities almost eliminated these infections, and Baptist won't stop until it achieves a rate of zero.

Plans

Most organizations have a strategic plan, and in most organizations the strategic plan is known by the executives throughout the organization but not translated to the front line. Translated to the front line means beyond the staff understanding the goals of the organization, but that they understand *how* they impact them. Taking it one step further, with Hoshin, they are part of continuous improvement and the ideas and solutions that are generated to help the hospital achieve its goals. Staff are problem solvers. They solve problems in their work life every day and naturally look for ways to optimize their workflow or "make their job easier." Think of what you could accomplish if your staff were working to achieve your facility strategic goals! You now have hundreds of problem solvers heading in the same direction moving the organization. Glass wall is similar to a component of Hoshin in that it communicates the hospital goals to the directors, and they in turn work on leading indicators on their unit to support it. However, glass wall metrics were not built into a timeline with goals throughout the organization's fiscal year. We like to say, "How much?" and "By when?" when working on Hoshin so that it's a manageable target, and we set goals that are

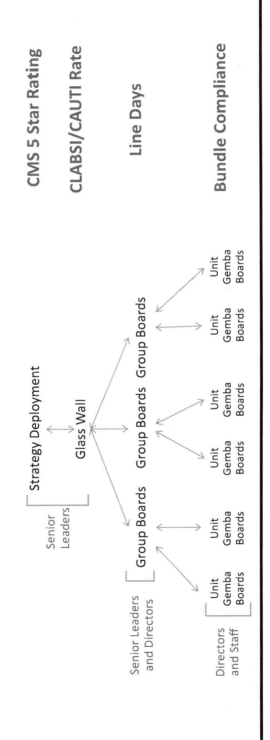

BHS Lean Management System: Plans

CMS 5 Star Rating

CLABSI/CAUTI Rate

Line Days

Bundle Compliance

Strategy Deployment

Glass Wall

Senior Leaders

Group Boards Group Boards Group Boards

Group Boards Group Boards

Unit Gemba Boards

Unit Gemba Boards

Unit Gemba Boards

Unit Gemba Boards

Unit Gemba Boards

Senior Leaders and Directors

Unit Gemba Boards

Directors and Staff

Figure 5.5 Group board example and associated metrics at each level.

realistic for the team. For example, with glass wall we did not set a goal that we would achieve $x\%$ reduction of infections by x time, nor were the goals woven into structured progress reviews. Glass wall served as an interim step for the facilities that now use Hoshin. Hoshin takes more time and more facilitators to bring on-line at a hospital and not all facilities were ready to do this; therefore, glass wall helped to serve as an interim step and a foundation for Hoshin.

Hoshin should cascade the goals of the organization through the executive leaders all the way to the front line and include catch-ball sessions along the way so that each level has the opportunity to set their goals that align with those of the organizations. At Baptist, when we moved from glass wall to Hoshin at select facilities, we implemented a modified Hoshin. We worked with the facilities on their annual priorities and targets based off the system goals. Then these goals were cascaded across the administrative team, where each team member set their goals to align with the facility targets. Subsequently, we cascaded the goals to directors and managers, who also set goals to support facility targets (Figure 5.6).

These goals and timelines were documented and reviewed monthly between the director and the executive, as well as between the executive and the CEO. These were somewhat of a progress review (a check-in). Instead of using the traditional x-matrix used in Hoshin, we utilized a simple Excel document. This came as the result of a session we held with one of the hospital leadership teams. We introduced the x-matrix and soon discovered that everyone was so concerned about the format of the document that they were forgetting the purpose of the document. *Lesson learned: Be flexible in your structure. Don't get hung up on the fact that you must use specific templates that cannot be modified. Support the purpose of what you are trying to achieve.* Therefore, this new Excel document became our template, and everyone was much more comfortable with interacting and updating it (Figure 5.7).

When we implemented Hoshin at a facility, we began with an executive session that consisted of the executive leadership team of the facility and one or two operational improvement engineers. The executive team consisted of the CEO, chief operating officer (COO), chief nursing officer (CNO), chief financial officer (CFO), chief human resources officer (CHRO), and chief growth officer (CGO). In this session, we provided education to the executive team on Hoshin and their individual roles and responsibilities. Prior to the session, the executive team was provided with an overview of Hoshin and what they needed to prepare. Individually, each executive

How It Works—The Process

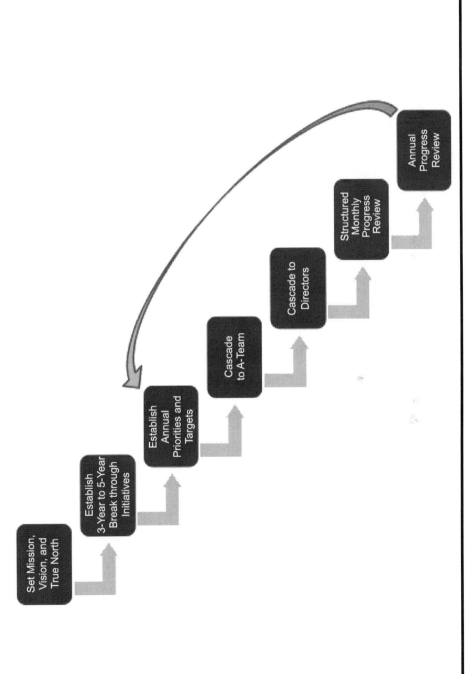

Set Mission, Vision, and True North

Establish 3-Year to 5-Year Break through Initiatives

Establish Annual Priorities and Targets

Cascade to A-Team

Cascade to Directors

Structured Monthly Progress Review

Annual Progress Review

Figure 5.6   Cascading Hoshin goals.

CEO Hoshin					How Much - By When				COO Hoshin			How Much - By When				Director Hoshin		
Pillar/ 2016 Goal	#	Category/ Target	Current YTD	What (Hospital Priorities)	Q1	Q2	Q3	Q4	Pillar Goal	Current	What (COO Priorities)	Q1	Q2	Q3	Q4	What (Director's Priorities)	Current	How Much - By When
Quality: Goal ____	1																	
	2																	
	3																	
	4																	
Service: Goal____	1																	
	2																	
	3																	
	4																	
Operations and People: Goal____	1																	
	2																	
	3																	
	4																	
	5																	
Growth: Goal ____	1																	
	2																	
	3																	
	4																	
Finance: Goal ____	1																	
	2																	
	3																	

○ = Exceeds
△ = Meets
⊗ = Does not meet

Figure 5.7 Baptist Hoshin form.

completed assignments prior to the session and the engineers completed prep work to ensure that all attendees would have a good understanding of the current state of the facility under each of the pillars (quality, operations, experience, growth, and finance). Additionally, other attendees who were subject matter experts (SMEs) were invited. For example, the system director of quality attended and reviewed a quality strengths, weaknesses, opportunities, and threats (SWOT) analysis with the leadership team. This executive session took from a half to a whole day, with the deliverable to have the facility's annual goals by pillars identified, along with quarterly targets. Furthermore, we reached agreement on the timeline for each stage of Hoshin and when each executive should have their Hoshin completed, as well as their direct reports.

Within one week of the executive session, the same engineers that were in the executive session met with the CEO, or president, of the facility. In this session, we reviewed the facility Hoshin that was just completed and worked with the CEO to develop their Hoshin. The CEO delineated their priorities that aligned with each facility goal and set target dates.

Within two weeks of the CEO session, the engineers met with each member of the executive team to work on their Hoshin. This usually consisted of multiple sessions, depending on if follow-up was required for metric research and target date setting. In each of these sessions, the Hoshin Excel document was updated accordingly and posted on the shared drive for access by the executive team.

Once the executive level of the Hoshin was completed, the department leader (director-level) catch-ball sessions could begin. Prior to the catch-ball sessions, we needed to educate the directors on Hoshin as well. Often, the facility held a director retreat, at which time we provided Hoshin education and the executives would review the overall facility goals and their individual Hoshin with the directors of the hospital. This was very effective in generating discussion across the various departments and in how they can support each other. Additionally, during these sessions we discussed activities that did not align with these facility goals and took time from our directors. From this, we made a list of things to stop doing. Within the following month, the directors had their catch-ball sessions with their executive to finalize their Hoshin goals and identified activities from the "stop doing" list that could be discontinued.

Remember fundamental number two, have fun! We always tried to have fun in these sessions and engaged the leaders in various activities that would stimulate discussion. The directors don't want to sit in an all-day education session that consists of slides! The likelihood of your audience learning, and remembering how to take the content and apply it, drops if they are not engaged. So, we engaged them in various ways, such as slides, skits, videos, team activities, and active discussion of their current issues. Just as we taught our leaders when doing gemba walks, we asked open-ended questions to increase discussion. At one session when we started Hoshin, we also incorporated the theme of the Oregon Trail. The wagon train was headed out West; just like Hoshin creates a "True North," we knew our "True West." Each wagon had to plan the use of its resources to ensure that it made it to Oregon without running out of supplies. We related this activity to Hoshin and how once you know the hospital strategic direction and priorities, you can plan your year to support these and timeline your activities and resource allocation appropriately.

As mentioned in Chapter 6, there are various waves and catch-ball sessions that conclude with the staff catch-ball sessions. At Baptist, we needed to modify this last step. We used an existing part of the management structure to help us augment the last element of Hoshin until we were able to reach that point in our journey. What element of the management system involved the frontline staff and could be leveraged to support the goals of the director? The unit-level gemba boards! Following the executive catch-ball session with their director, the engineer would work with the director to incorporate the gemba board and identify how the board could support the director's goals. This often meant pulling in frontline team members to determine what metrics they should be working on, and if they needed to be monitoring, problem solving, or experimenting (Figure 5.8 through 5.10).

Why did we modify the Hoshin process at Baptist from its true form and the structured catch-ball sessions? I return to fundamental number one I mentioned earlier: understand the current environment and what would be the best fit. When we started Hoshin, certain facilities in the system were very eager but could commit a limited amount of resources (staff time) to the deployment. Additionally, for Baptist Health System we had to utilize the current staff of three engineers wisely, as they supported approximately 7000 employees. This did not mean that the CEO was not supportive of Hoshin or Lean, but we had parameters to work within just like our directors or engineers in the many process improvement projects they work on every day. Knowing the limitations we had with fully deploying all elements of Hoshin, we contemplated holding off on deployment, but then we considered the opportunity we would be missing to take yet another step forward with our management system. Understanding the parameters we needed to work within, the operational improvement team developed plans with each

LDM integration with strategy

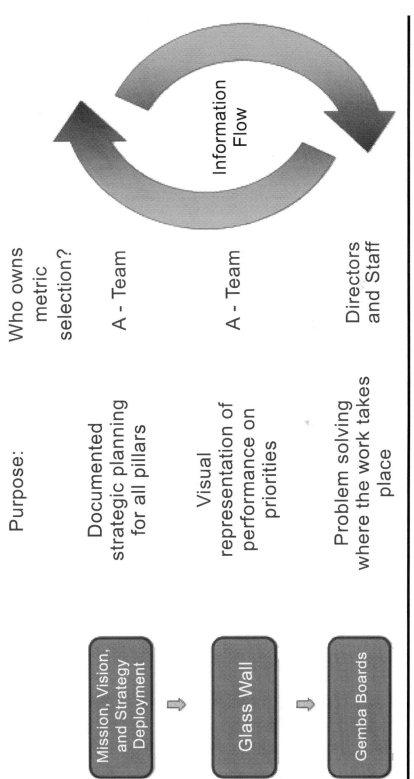

	Purpose:	Who owns metric selection?
Mission, Vision, and Strategy Deployment	Documented strategic planning for all pillars	A - Team
Glass Wall	Visual representation of performance on priorities	A - Team
Gemba Boards	Problem solving where the work takes place	Directors and Staff

Information Flow

Figure 5.8   LDM integration and metric ownership.

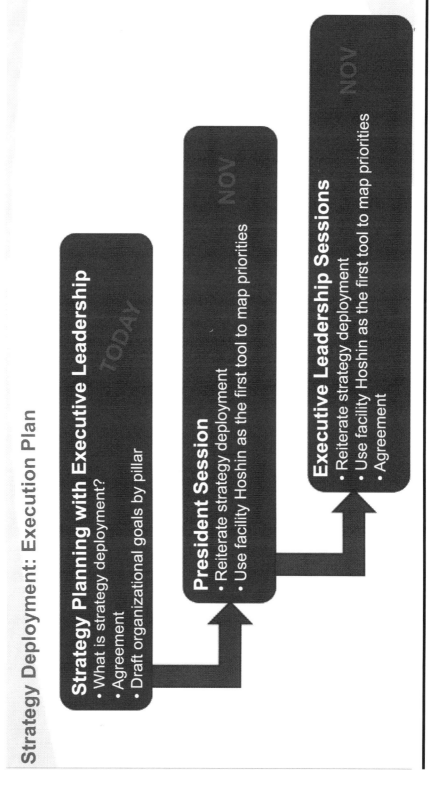

Figure 5.9 Strategy deployment execution plan: executive leadership.

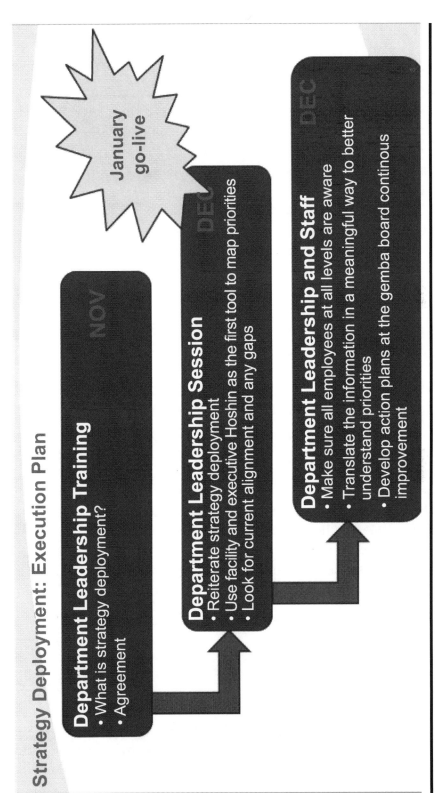

Figure 5.10 Strategy deployment execution plan: departmental leadership.

of the CEOs, at three of the six hospitals, that would both support and keep us moving forward on our Hoshin journey.

Another important factor to consider when setting out on your Hoshin journey is the organizational structure of your facility and its human resources department or division. Are you a stand-alone hospital or part of a larger system? Is human resources managed locally or at a corporate level? This may affect your ability to more readily modify your personnel evaluation structure and fully incorporate Hoshin. If you are incorporating Hoshin into the performance evaluation system, it will take more time if you need to modify a larger system structure versus a facility.

At Baptist, during our Hoshin deployment we were acquired by another system and chose to not pursue incorporating Hoshin into the evaluation structure at that time. The specific evaluation goals were not modified in the performance system. However, Hoshin could be added as supporting documentation for a more generic performance standard that already existed in the staff performance evaluations related to participating in performance improvement activities.

What is beautiful about Hoshin is that you have a plan and you are not alone on how you are going to reach the objectives of your plan! You, as the CEO, are not alone! You, as the director and frontline employee, are not alone either!

Of course, Hoshin helped our directors plan and prioritize for the year. One of the COOs would tell his directors, "I know you have a lot of plates spinning in the air; if you need to drop something, don't let it be something tied to these goals on your Hoshin." This was comforting to the directors; they would tell me, "At least I know my priorities and that everything can't be the priority." Hoshin helped me as a market leader to plan where the market office would support the facilities with a kaizen or other targeted improvement efforts. Having planned for the resources made it easier to respond to the on-demand needs, which always come up in healthcare.

Lessons Learned

I've mentioned several of the lessons that we learned throughout the years of our journey. For me, the importance of coaching and being flexible are probably the most important lessons learned for us at Baptist. Never miss an opportunity to coach someone, and don't assume that your executives or middle-level management are comfortable in how to coach others. You will need to help them through this. To engage all levels in continuous improvement, you must treat people with respect, coach them, and *listen* to their ideas.

Additionally, there are many tools, templates, and opinions on how Lean should be deployed, but make sure to design your deployment on your organizational needs. Not all of our facilities were ready for Hoshin (three of the six hospitals began Hoshin). Remember, it is not just a deployment, but rather, it is a journey! Each of the elements in the management system at Baptist can exist separately, but the likelihood of the success of the management system strengthens when these are all present. For me, it would have been very hard to begin strategy deployment (Hoshin) without the other three elements of the management system in place. However, I would like to have started with glass wall at the same time as the gemba walks so there would have been more coordination of efforts early on and the link to Hoshin would have been made earlier.

Don't get hung up on formalities, for example, the time and frequency the leadership team rounds on the unit. This frequency should depend on the needs of the facility and the leadership team strength and style. Don't force them to walk the same units every day if they can rotate their rounds on a different schedule and get the same outcome. You don't want to lose their support totally by being overly prescriptive early on. Instead, be flexible and match the needs to the demand of the particular process and department. What is important is that the leaders are going to the gemba, where the work is done, on some schedule, and engaging and supporting the front line while supporting their directors to do the same.

Use templates they are likely to use. For example, if you get a team engaged and supportive of Hoshin, don't demand that they must use an x-matrix template; use whatever template they understand, and that increases the likelihood that they will use it. A beautiful x-matrix that sits dormant and not updated isn't beautiful at all!

While it hasn't been the perfect journey, we learned from our mistakes and celebrated many wins together. Baptist Health System has a structure that supports continuous improvement and engages individuals throughout the organization, but as mentioned earlier in the book, this is a journey, and it will continue to improve upon this and further its management system, including Hoshin. When I think of Baptist's Lean journey over the past 10 years, I think of *Shu-Ha-Ri*. I learned about the term *Shu-Ha-Ri* from one of the great engineers I worked with at Baptist. *Shu-Ha-Ri* comes from Japanese martial arts and describes the stages of learning. *Shu* is the first phase, where the student complies very strictly with the form they are taught

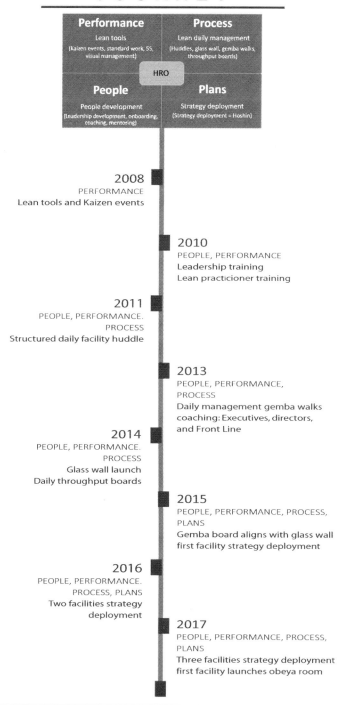

Figure 5.11   Baptist Lean journey.

by their teacher and do not vary their technique from their teacher's instruction. *Ha* is the second phase, where the student has learned the basic forms and begins to learn more of the principles and theory behind the form, as well as starts learning from other teachers. *Ri* is the final phase, where instead of learning from other teachers, the student learns from themselves and modifies their technique to their abilities and environment. Baptist started on a Lean journey (Figure 5.11) almost 10 years ago, and each time it implemented a new element of the management system, it went through these phases. Baptist adhered strictly to form, learned the principles, and then made it its own, and when Baptist made it its own is when it had the greatest success.

Chapter 6

Hoshin Timelines

Hoshin Kanri planning requires clear timelines so that everyone's goals (catch-ball sessions) are aligned and completed as effectively and timely as possible. One to two months prior to strategy development and our initial C-level Hoshin catch-ball sessions, the combined human resources (HR), quality, and process improvement catch-ball facilitator team needs to prepare to train the three key "waves" of catch-ball sessions down through the organization. Additionally, this team will need to tightly schedule and coordinate which leaders each of them will deliver Hoshin training or refresher training to and facilitate catch-ball sessions with. It's best to set up specific time frames for each hospital, where the entire team will be coming through to support the three catch-ball setting waves (wave 1, C-level to vice president or director; wave 2, director to frontline supervisor; and wave 3, supervisor to frontline staff). Give yourself enough time in your Hoshin deployment schedule to pick up leaders that may have been out on vacation or absent for another reason.

The hospital or system CEO and hospital or system senior HR executive should set these timelines and communicate this to all leaders and staff. It's the responsibility of all leaders to sign up for their Hoshin training and to coordinate with their catch-ball facilitator to compete their Hoshin goals. Most leaders will wait until the very last minute to get their catch-ball sessions scheduled and accomplished, thereby placing a tremendous pressure on our catch-ball facilitators to get everyone completed in a crunch that can affect the quality of the catch-ball sessions. Your senior HR executive needs to be the Hoshin champion and manage the three waves of Hoshin training and catch-ball sessions very closely. *Lesson learned: It's a good idea to have your senior HR executives present at key Hoshin catch-ball kick-off sessions and ongoing progress sessions to make sure that all leaders show up, are engaged, and meet their Hoshin timelines.*

Your Hoshin champion (typically your senior HR executive or chief strategy officer) is communicating and managing the Hoshin process from initial strategy development to C-level catch-ball goal-setting sessions and all the way down the organization to ensure that catch-ball sessions are timely, meaningful, measurable, and aligned. Synchronizing your Hoshin timelines for each of these phases with the facilitator schedule to support each phase will be key to a successful rollout and your annual Hoshin process.

Hoshin Prep

C-level leaders need to schedule at least two or three catch-ball sessions ahead of time with each of their vice presidents or directors and send their personal Hoshin forms (with their Hoshin goals completed) to their direct reports in advance of each catch-ball session to ensure that the goal-setting session is meaningful. Directors and above will need refresher Hoshin training (30 minutes to 1 hour) ahead of their very first catch-ball sessions (this training can be offered as a webinar to help reach leaders faster, but it's recommended that the first time a leader learns and practices Hoshin, it should be with an experienced Hoshin facilitator). In addition to scheduling of C-level leaders, directors, frontline supervisors, and staff, be sure to schedule your Hoshin catch-ball facilitators, as well to ensure proper coverage. (Try to align HR, quality, and process improvement catch-ball facilitators with those areas they are normally used to supporting or already have key relationships with, and build a schedule for these catch-ball facilitators to be available for their leaders.)

Wave 1: C-Level to Vice President– or Director-Level Catch-Ball Sessions (Set the Tone for Hoshin)

C-level (senior leadership) catch-ball sessions need to happen in less than two weeks and by your best catch-ball facilitators. C-level Hoshin training needs to happen first (even after your first year of implementation) to ensure that senior leaders still understand and stay true to the Hoshin process (new leaders will inevitably enter the organization, so they will need to learn and understand the Hoshin process). As senior leadership develops their strategy, Hoshin catch-ball sessions and goal setting should be included in this process so there's not too much of a time gap between your C-level catch-ball sessions and the initial development of organizational strategy (the strategy is still fresh in senior leadership's mind).

Wave 2: Director-Level to Supervisor Catch-Ball Sessions

As senior leadership completes their C-level catch-ball sessions and Hoshin goals with their vice presidents and directors, the following month is dedicated to director-level and above catch-ball sessions, which cascade down from our C-level Hoshin goals and Hoshin form or worksheet. The earlier an organization can schedule catch-ball sessions, the better, to ensure a seamless cascading of goals from the C-level to the director and then to frontline supervisors and staff. Scheduling catch-ball sessions in real time is often too difficult, and the whole process winds up taking much longer and is much more frustrating for staff than it should be.

Wave 3: Frontline Supervisor to Staff Catch-Ball Sessions

As directors and frontline supervisors establish their Hoshin goals, the final step is to cascade those goals from frontline supervisors to staff. You will need at least two to three months to complete this step (depending on the organization and/or department size). Frontline staff will need just-in-time Hoshin training as well, to ensure that they understand why Hoshin is so important to them and the organization. This training can be delivered by the frontline director or supervisor or using one of your Hoshin facilitators. It's very important to *not* skip this training of frontline staff on Hoshin, as this group is "where the rubber meets the road," so to speak. The Hoshin training and goal-setting (catch-ball) timeline and expectations (as well as supporting material and catch-ball forms) should come from your HR team well in advance of your annual Hoshin process. Establishing a Hoshin hotline, along with prescheduled Hoshin training sessions to send leaders and staff to so they can learn or refresh, can help streamline the Hoshin process (as opposed to a reactive process for reaching catch-ball facilitators).

Supervisor to frontline staff Hoshin catch-ball sessions happen best one on one. However, with the sheer volume of staff a supervisor may have across various shifts, catch-ball sessions can also happen in groups that have similar goals. As an example, a director of the emergency department (ED) may have one manager, four or five charge nurses, several triage or intake nurses, trauma nurses, techs, and so forth. Each of these groups may have unique Hoshin goals that align to the supervisor's and director's goals (i.e., intake nurse cycle time goal of less than five minutes, charge nurse goal of ED length of stay for nonadmitted patients of less than two hours, etc.). Hoshin goals allow each ED staff member alignment in their particular role (day shift, night shift, triage RN, charge RN, etc.) to the overall goals of the ED, whether it is related to ED length of stay, quality of care, patient experience, or labor management. Hoshin goals give the ED staff alignment, clarity, and a sense of focus in an otherwise chaotic environment. These specific Hoshin goals make it very clear who is accountable and working on key aspects of our ED. Frontline Hoshin goals also helps staff "connect the dots" from the work they do day to day on the floor to their hospital- and system-level strategies and goals, giving more purpose and meaning to their goals and work.

Perioperative Services Operating Room Frontline Supervisor to Staff Hoshin Goal Setting

The operating room (OR) is another area that has many staff that have uniquely different goals. OR charge nurses, OR circulators, sterile processing techs, and other staff all come together like an orchestra to attempt to provide the highest-quality, safest, most efficient care possible with the best possible patient experience and outcomes. Each of these groups of OR staff may have their own unique Hoshin goals that align to their supervisor's and director's goals. Charge nurses may have Hoshin goals such as on-time or first-case starts or cost per case. OR directors may have Hoshin goals related to block utilization, OR room utilization, and/or OR volume. OR techs may have goals related to OR room turnaround times, sterile processing may have Hoshin goals around flash rates, and so forth. Everyone in the OR understands how their goals align with each other, their leaders, their unit Lean daily management or huddle board, and the organization's strategy. This is very powerful!

Who Really Owns the Goals in Your Organization?

Many leaders and staff will state that they already have such goals in place and track these measures, so why spend the time and energy to align and cascade to all staff? The reality is that the director and supervisor wind up "owning" all of these goals and staff doesn't truly own any of them. I've spent many years in healthcare working with many a burned-out ED director or OR director who worked tirelessly to try to engage and hold accountable all his or her frontline staff with such goals and could not get the kind of consistent accountability to make these goals stick. Staff need to understand and see how their individual OR goals align not only to those of their supervisors and director, but also, more importantly, back to hospital and system-level goals and strategies in a very clear way. Toyota understands this breakdown in goals from senior leadership to the frontline staff and created the Hoshin process to address this gap.

In this OR example, the Hoshin process forces the director and supervisor to think very deeply about what key goals the OR needs to be successful with their boss and that hospital's strategic goals (over the course of two or three catch-ball sessions, pulling data and getting very clear about what's realistic with goals and what's not) and then cascades those goals (using catch-ball sessions) from the director to the supervisor to key frontline staff members and key frontline staff groups that may have similar goals. The rigor of the Hoshin process itself engages the frontline staff member in the goal-setting process in a way that most have never engaged in before. It forces the frontline staff member to think more deeply about their individual goals and how they align with those of their supervisor. Staff members can now easily connect the dots, using the Hoshin form, from their individual goals to their supervisor's goals to their director's goals to their chief nursing officer's goals to their CEO or president's goals, and then ultimately to their market goals and their system goals and strategies. The Hoshin process creates greater buy-in to goals because it pulls frontline staff directly (front and center) into the goal-setting process, compared with traditional goal-setting and performance management processes that do not cascade down the frontline nurse level very well at all. Nurses today often feel very disconnected from key hospital and strategic goals because these goals don't have clear alignment to them personally.

Chapter 7

Hoshin Change Management

The Hoshin process will initially feel like one more extra thing leaders and staff must do since they already have, in most cases, an existing goal-setting process as part of their annual reviews.

> *Tip 1*: Staff listen to their immediate supervisors for the "real" message and explanations of what change means to them. Spend plenty of time with your frontline supervisors to ensure that the message is clear.
>
> *Tip 2*: Make it easy for both frontline supervisors and the CEO by creating scripted messages or frequently asked questions (FAQs) and corresponding answers for their staff. Make sure to address "What's in it for me?" (WIIFM) for leaders and staff as well.

So, what is in it for leaders and staff anyhow? How does Hoshin help everyone? How is it different from what we already do? How will it help me with my patients, my workday, and my ability to grow and be successful in my organization?

Hoshin Ethos, Pathos, and Logos (Learning from the Early Greeks to Help Us with Hoshin Change Management)

The answers to these questions must come from the right people first and foremost! Follow the age-old Greek orator process (Aristotle coined the terms) of ethos first (ethics), then pathos (emotion) and logos (logic). The old orators of Greece had to have ethos first and foremost for the audience to even listen to what they had to say (ethics + credibility + respect + trust). Who in your organization has the most credibility? It's not always those with the highest rank or title. In most hospitals, your chief nursing officers may have the most ethos since they represent the largest functional group of staff in the hospital, which are nurses. In other hospitals, it may be a well-respected and trusted chief operating officer. At the unit level, it may be a supervisor that everyone respects. Enlist these folks to help bring ethos to your Hoshin message!

Once you've got the right people to get your leaders and staff to listen (ethos), you will need the right emotional message (*pathos* is the Greek word for suffering and experience). Using meaningful language, emotional tone, emotion-evoking examples, stories of emotional events, and implied meanings can develop pathos. In most hospitals, e-mail is usually not the best channel for communicating new behavioral changes and a powerful emotional message. Face-to-face delivery methods are always preferred, supported by webinars and videos. Hoshin town halls continually let staff know that this is important over time and can reconnect the emotion of our mission to our Hoshin process. Stories and messages of connection and alignment to our patients, mission, and values using the Hoshin process give it greater emotional appeal to our leaders and staff. The dangers or risk of disconnection from our patients, mission, and values without our Hoshin process evokes different emotions as well.

The logic (logos), or "how to," of Hoshin now has credibility and a clear emotional message and connection for leaders and staff to plug into and understand what must be done.

Following the ethos, pathos, and logos method doesn't guarantee that every staff member will understand or buy into the Hoshin process; however, it does increase the probability of successful goal-setting sessions (catch-ball sessions) and integration into our existing performance review process. All Hoshin training, FAQs, webinars, videos, and training and coaching build and align with the Hoshin ethos, pathos, and logos foundation you've built. Over time, the best change management will come from those leaders and staff that have used the Hoshin process and realized the benefits, and can advocate and help educate on the Hoshin process.

Defining Hoshin WIIFM for Leaders and Staff

So, what is the WIIFM for leaders and staff when it comes to Hoshin? Most hospital leaders and staff feel very detached from the hospital strategies, goals, and metrics, which either leaves them feeling powerless to truly make a measurable difference or creates a false sense of security that if there's no one yelling, all must be well in the hospital today, this week, or this month. Meanwhile, your hospital continues to get either better or worse irrespective of frontline staff engagement toward key organizational goals.

Never underestimate the power of individual pride, friendly competition, and daily measurement! Every one of your staff brings individual strengths that you need to understand and tap into. *Aligning those individual strengths to key unit and organizational goals through the Hoshin process unleashes something deeper within that individual that neither you nor they ever realized they had or were capable of!*

Most staff are aware of their weaknesses. Supervisors, family members, peers, and others remind them of their weaknesses (actively or passively) every day. This daily reinforcement of individual weaknesses can build up to the point where many simply give up on trying to develop and harness their strengths and spend most of their time trying not to fail or expose their weaknesses. Their ego becomes fragile and must be protected at all cost, so they avoid "new things" and failure at all costs. It takes a very strong ego to try new things, fail, learn what worked and what didn't, and try again. We need to remember that as leaders working to drive meaningful change and develop our people and organizations!

As with any change, leaders and staff need to know what tasks or activities will come off their plate to make time for Hoshin goal setting or catch-ball sessions. Leaders and staff will need to know not only *why* it's important to their hospital and them personally, but also *how* it will fit into their already overwhelming schedule.

Hoshin implementation requires deeper respect for staff's time. Catch-ball goal-setting sessions need to be well thought through and crisp, which requires patience, preparation, and practice. Catch-ball sessions that take much longer than planned can be perceived as wasteful, so plan ahead! Remember, every minute our catch-ball sessions take staff off the floor is time they could be spending with a patient.

Offering Hoshin "prework" for leaders and staff raises the probability of successful catch-ball sessions. Hoshin prework can be human resources (HR) webinars or training modules, FAQs with answers, and Hoshin examples. For key functional roles, such as nurses, physicians, and Environmental Services (EVS), give specific examples that are relevant to their particular nature of work. Webinars or training modules should use real staff from key areas to walk through the specific examples. Make Hoshin yours! Weave in those key cultural pieces that will make Hoshin sound and feel like part of your organizational culture.

Many leaders and staff will need to understand why their current goal-setting process is failing or falling short (for the organization and for them personally) before they will consider adopting Hoshin. The CEO is usually the best person to deliver this message face-to-face in a town hall–type setting. Great examples of how unaligned and broken our existing goal-setting process and strategy deployment process are are all around us! In radiology, for example, their goals are typically focused on optimizing their specific functions, which may or may not be aligned with their key customers. Radiology may have specific goals to improve outpatient volume and growth, but nothing specific to align and support inpatient throughput and the emergency department (ED). This puts added stress on the radiology team because while they may meet departmental goals, key customers, like the ED, telemetry, or med-surg, continue to miss their throughput goals in part due to the failure of radiology to align and support them effectively.

Do We Really Need More Staff or Better Alignment?

Sometimes the answer isn't more equipment, technology, resources, or staff, but better alignment of goals through Hoshin-style goal setting. At a system level, Hoshin aligns hospitals, specialty clinics, and free-standing EDs toward regional and system goals leveraging each hospital and ED's strengths to meet broader system goals (as opposed to competing with each other, as is common in most health systems). Many health system hospitals compete with each other and cannibalize physicians and patients from each other versus aligning themselves to leverage their individual strengths.

System and regional Hoshin goals truly clarify each hospital's strengths (key service lines, talent, etc.) in a way that allows each hospital in the system to complement the others. Currently, most system-level leaders and staff work furiously to support their regional and local hospitals with quality, growth, voluntary nurse turnover, labor management, and patient satisfaction goals, but usually fall short because every regional hospital is working on these goals independently and there is very little synergy or alignment hospital to hospital or even hospital to region or system. Additionally, there is often a good deal of overlap and waste in many hospital-level, regional-level, and system-level leader and support staff roles. Hoshin ensures that you are not wasting precious time and labor on unaligned positions at the hospital, regional, and system level (which can drive labor cost up significantly). The Hoshin process creates that alignment taking into consideration each hospital's strengths, weaknesses, opportunities, and threats (SWOT).

In a similar way, Hoshin changes the way units work with each other. When unit director and staff goals are aligned and pointing to tough goals, such as length of stay (LOS) (of a patient in the hospital), *Clostridium difficile* infections, or patient satisfaction scores, those goals start to move in a way that never occurred before. The Hoshin process aligns leaders and staff to the hospital's toughest cross-functional goals, like LOS, through intense goal-setting catch-ball sessions where every department, leader, and staff member that ties into that goal aligns themselves to LOS within the functional work they do (i.e., EVS Hoshin goal to focus on cleaning rooms for discharging patients at key times of the day, radiology Hoshin goal to focus on discharging patients at key times of the day, and hospitalist Hoshin goal to focus on discharging patients earlier in the day).

Daily huddle boards give each department, leader, and staff member a visual way of tracking, managing, and improving these aligned Hoshin LOS goals. Creating a daily cadence on LOS with these key huddle boards and aligned Hoshin goals accelerates movement of LOS goals by placing accountability on those key units, leaders, and staff to problem-solve daily. Leadership rounds on these LOS huddle boards escalate LOS barriers daily and drive actions for improvement. There is no "silver bullet" for reducing LOS in our hospitals and keeping it there. It's a combination of leading (vs. lagging) LOS metrics, aligned Hoshin goals across the right staff and units, daily huddle board tracking, management and improvement on these goals, and effective leadership rounding on LOS huddle boards to drive daily problem solving and accountability on LOS goals.

Hoshin Kanri, like so many Toyota methods, isn't complex, but it is very challenging to implement effectively and consistently (like so many Toyota methods, it's more of a practice than a simple tool). Leaders at Toyota grow up in Toyota learning and practicing the Toyota Production System, or the "Toyota Way."

Toyota, much like our U.S. military, spends a lot of time and money on the development of its leaders and staff from within. You cannot become a general in the U.S. Army if you haven't already served in the U.S. Army as a junior officer, proven yourself as a leader in the field, and learned the U.S. Army's customs and culture, and aren't able to teach and coach others on the U.S. Army's customs and culture, as well as key standard operating procedures (essentially the "U.S. Army Way"). This is important to note because in most U.S. organizations, new leaders often bring in their own set of best practices instead of trying to understand or learn what practices are already in place. This creates a never-ending cycle of "churn," where no one truly understands what his or her organizational standard practices and processes truly are. It also adds to the well-justified and epidemic "program of the month" mentality. To add to the churn as profits drop below expectations, we often blame the CEO primarily and not the system or processes they work within, and yet another leader is brought in to redefine our organizational processes and practices.

The Toyota Way (which includes Hoshin planning) is set in place and doesn't change with a new CEO. The direction of the organization may change, but Hoshin goal setting still happens.

CEOs or presidents of hospitals have to show profits fairly quickly, which often leaves very little time for true long-lasting process improvement or development of leaders and staff. As a new CEO comes in, they quickly bring in their key leaders and focus on the most obvious expenses and revenue areas: labor and growth. This new team has a limited time to show results (profits) before they are then replaced. This cycle continues for years, and the result is an entirely eroded infrastructure (MRI machines that are operating on their last leg, high staff turnover in key areas like the ED and intensive care unit, completely broken processes, lots of work-arounds, and seemingly unsolvable quality issues).

The interesting thing is that this is exactly where Toyota was many years ago. Toyota realized that it needed to do something different, so it studied and learned from many sources—and still does! Toyota's goals were and still are very long term, not just annually or quarterly, which forces the organization and its leaders to focus on infrastructure, not just quarterly profits. We've read about SMART (specific, measurable, actionable, realistic, and timely) goals in an earlier chapter, but this last piece, timeliness, is key. Hoshin planning forces us to start thinking longer term, which then results in us looking at longer-term strategies, which attracts a different kind of leader, who in turn builds a different (longer-term thinking and planning) organization. Certainly, there are short-term strategies and tactics to meet key financial goals; however, there is still focus on longer-term strategies to keep the organization strong and competitive.

Annual Hoshin Preparation

Establishing a clear timeline for strategy development and deployment, and Hoshin training and development for directors and above, and then frontline supervisors and staff, is key. Catch-ball sessions are quite different than traditional goal-setting sessions and can sometimes take two or three iterations to get the most leading goals and measures. Most leaders and staff will try to rush through this process and get back to their "real" work. It's important to prepare as many catch-ball session coaches as needed to support the numerous catch-ball sessions that will cascade down from C-level to directors, and then to frontline supervisors and their staff. Partnering with HR, quality, and other key support groups can help bring more resources to support effective catch-ball or goal-setting sessions.

Developing "Hoshin Heroes"

Each of these Hoshin catch-ball session coaches becomes uniquely qualified to facilitate effective goal-setting sessions. It's actually OK when the catch-ball coach doesn't have deep experience with the areas they support, because it forces the manager and staff members to be very clear on the goal, how it aligns to key strategies, and how it will be measured. These catch-ball coaches get better and better with each and every Hoshin cycle (annually). They form camaraderie after years of facilitating goal-setting sessions and become more valuable to the leaders and functional areas they serve and support.

This core of catch-ball "facilitators" gain better insight into what high-level and frontline goals their functional areas have and often are able to weave their support into many of these key functional goals (HR recruiting more effectively knowing customer goals in more depth, quality preventing harm more effectively knowing their customer goals in greater depth, and process improvement implementing more aligned and impactful Lean Six Sigma projects). Support areas like HR, quality, and continuous improvement are embraced as partners like never before with their operational customers. Hoshin brings the organization closer together as it moves through the Hoshin process. Facilitators start to "see" how to help connect the dots across many siloed functional areas or units and hospitals because they are facilitating so many catch-ball goal-setting sessions across so many groups. Facilitators help prevent overlapping or opposing or unaligned goals across functional areas that may not normally communicate well with each other.

The process of Hoshin is not easy. Hoshin forces leaders and staff to stretch themselves a bit to find even more leading measures and goals to achieve their key goals and strategies. Your core Hoshin facilitator team of HR, quality, process improvement, and others will need lots of encouragement, recognition, and some key celebrations to remind them of the value they've created, because the organization may not completely feel like this work is valuable at first. Celebrating key milestones and results keeps the team and organization inspired to continue on and improve next year's Hoshin process. Something as simple as aligning our ED goals with lab, radiology, registration, and other key areas is a great reason for celebration with these traditionally siloed groups.

Southwest Airlines tells the story of how its baggage handlers on the front lines can explain to anyone how getting bags off the planes and on the carousel in less than 25 minutes ensures that they are doing their part to achieve their key strategy of being the most reliable on-time airline in the industry. It's a point of pride and not an accident. Southwest Airlines ensures that all staff goals are easily and effectively aligned to their strategies, which is one key reason it remains a leader in its industry.

Gaps in Hoshin

Hoshin Kanri, like so many Lean methods, is more of a practice than a series of forms and tools. Practicing Hoshin Kanri in healthcare has its share of gaps to overcome.

Gap 1: Hoshin Can Feel Like Extra Work to Leaders and Staff

Hoshin will feel like added work to leaders and staff that are used to less rigorous goal-setting, tracking, and management processes. Hoshin will also seem like a "throwback" to some because of the x-matrix forms many organizations use initially versus the automated performance management systems they may have in place. HR leaders and staff can perceive Hoshin as a "threat" to their existing goal-setting process and technology as well. It will be important to partner with HR early on in the process to gain understanding and buy-in.

Gap 2: Finding Time for Hoshin

Leaders will struggle to make time to not only complete Hoshin goals but also regularly review Hoshin goal progress with staff. In healthcare, the demand placed on clinicians to meet regulatory requirements, patient rounds, labor management and productivity standards, and quality requirements can be overwhelming, so communicating how Hoshin (or any Lean method for that matter) can help with these demands will be key. Pulling in HR, quality, patient experience, and key clinical leaders to first understand the Hoshin process and then help communicate the Hoshin *why* and WIIFM message to nursing (the largest functional group in the hospital) will dramatically improve your chances of Hoshin adoption.

Gap 3: Measuring Hoshin Successes and Benefits Isn't Always Easy

Hoshin isn't something that is always easy to measure in a way that clinical and nonclinical staff may appreciate. In the short term, Hoshin catch-ball sessions and training will actually pull staff away from time with their patients and clinical work to develop SMART, aligned goals. As an engineer, I am still learning to lead with nurses and physicians (clinicians) as much as I can and make sure the "engineers" are not the face of performance improvement. Hoshin needs a clinical champion as well as an HR champion. For any Lean method to "stick," leaders and staff need to see the benefits (intrinsic value). Goal alignment may mean something to leaders and engineers, but its benefits are not very compelling to a busy nurse on the hospital floor. What most clinicians would recognize as a benefit is for all the supporting staff (lab, radiology, pharmacy, etc.) to be working as a team toward aligned goals. Most nurses can tell you that certain lab and radiology staff do behave as a team and support them throughout the day; however, many will tell you that it's not always consistent and that it varies from shift to shift. Hoshin goals keep everyone aligned and accountable to each other, just like all strong teams behave. How can a team work together consistently if their goals aren't aligned?

Gap 4: Rolling Out Hoshin Too Broadly Too Fast

Although at a surface level Hoshin may seem simple, it's harder in practice, which is why we recommend a pilot hospital or model line approach to start. A model line approach helps your organization understand the x-matrix, catch-ball-style goal-setting and alignment sessions and goal management within a fixed group of people. The model line approach also helps your process improvement department, HR, and other Hoshin coaches understand what the demand on their time and staff's time will look like.

Taking Hoshin across the organization all at once is a huge endeavor with high risk. Focusing Hoshin on a key service line, such as the ED service line (ED, lab, radiology, pharmacy, transportation, access, EVS, etc.), can have a great impact with much less implementation risk. Once you've established Hoshin in a service line, leaders and staff can visit and "see" how Hoshin works and what it means for leaders and staff in that service line, as well as benefits it's brought (alignment of departments and people through Hoshin-style goal setting, tracking, and management).

Gap 5: Data

Many Hoshin goals will require data that may not be easily pulled from your electronic medical record (EMR) system. Aligning goals is the first step; getting the data to support ongoing performance will take additional support. Let's use the ED service line example to understand how data will come into play. At a high level, the hospital leadership has to establish their ED strategy and goals.

The ED service line is a great example of how Hoshin can align such diverse functional groups in arguably the most dynamic area in the hospital to consistently meet key ED goals and deliver optimal care and world-class patient experience. Currently, all these ED goals are tracked and managed (often not managed well) by the ED director and manager, with very little alignment of support departments, such as lab, radiology, and transport, and inconsistent alignment and support from medical staff. This situation creates overwhelming anxiety and stress for the ED director and manager to track and manage everything, and can ultimately lead to burnout and turnover in these key positions.

As each of these ED service line goals is established, each of the metrics and goals will need supporting data to track and manage each of the functional groups. This data is often more leading and a bit different from the lagging data and metrics your EMR standard reports may generate today. You may have to partner with your information management department to help pull some of the data you need for these new Hoshin goals.

Hoshin for Healthcare Hansei or Reflection

Practicing Lean methods in healthcare (by far the most complex, challenging, yet rewarding industry I have ever worked in) has been a series of plan–do–check–act (PDCA) cycles with many experiments and failures (which have taught me so much) and some successes. Applying Lean in healthcare has reinforced the need for goal clarity and alignment across the organization, from the CEO to the frontline nurse dealing with patients every day.

As reimbursements continue to decline, costs continue to rise, and demand continues to grow, clinicians and nonclinical staff will have even more pressure to improve labor costs and productivity, expenses, patient satisfaction, quality, and other key regulatory measures. Every employee and supplier in the hospital or health system needs to be 100% aligned and crystal clear on their Hoshin goals to meet the next 10 years of change in healthcare. Healthcare will need to move from a hero culture with great firefighters to a culture of execution or excellence and fire prevention, with everyone in the hospital aligned and engaged. Hospitals and health systems that continue to operate in silos, without Hoshin Kanri and Lean daily management in place to align goals and create a daily cadence for improvement across all staff, will significantly struggle. Those hospitals that are able to build Hoshin and Lean daily management into their culture will not only survive but also start to attract the best and brightest who wish to be part of a creative, innovative, and learning organization.

Index

Page numbers followed by f and t indicate figures and tables, respectively.